# BASKETBALL STRENGTH

## VOLUME 1

### DAVID LEMANCZYK

ISBN: 979-8-89031-883-1 (sc)
ISBN: 979-8-89031-884-8 (hc)
ISBN: 979-8-89031-885-5 (e)

Because of the dynamic nature of the Internet, any web addresses or links contained in this book may have changed since publication and may no longer be valid. The views expressed in this work are solely those of the author and do not necessarily reflect the views of the publisher, and the publisher hereby disclaims any responsibility for them.

THE EWINGS PUBLISHING

One Galleria Blvd., Suite 1900, Metairie, LA 70001
(504) 702-6708

# NOTICE

Please consult your primary care physician before attempting any of the Basketball Strength exercises detailed in this professional product, Volume I. The training system detailed within this book is not intended to replace a specific routine set in place by your medical doctor.

Basketball Strength Volume I is a rigorous course of physical exercise that is effort based and requires a competent level of fitness. Team Integrity Productions, www.basketballstrength.com, and David J. Lemanczyk are not liable for any injuries that may take place on behalf of any participants during Basketball Strength conditioning.

Please exercise at your own risk, listen to your body and only train when you are ready to. Make sure your training intensity and frequency accommodates your lifestyle. Enjoy the progressions of the Volume I conditioning methods, supplementary exercises and follow each Phase exactly as shown.

# DEDICATION

Basketball Strength Volume I is especially dedicated to my former teammates, coaches, and opponents. Without your participation and competition I would have never had such a fine measuring stick as to success. I appreciate the wealth of knowledge you have exposed and allotted me.

I would also like to send a special wish of luck and good fortune to all the hard working ballers/coaches across the planet past and present. Play hard, play smart, train no quarter, and play for the love of the game. Keep your intentions pure on the court and all things associated with. Good things will happen in time no matter how tough some situations may seem.

I would like to thank my wife for supporting me through endless nights of training, studying and writing. I am truly lucky to have a wife that is as caring as she.

A special thank you to my right hand man Chris Schrade for all his hard work and determination.

A thank you must be sent to Steve Weiner, Pat Povilaitis, and Team Integrity for all their support. Team Integrity represents an outstanding group of individuals dedicated to preserving the foundation of personal integrity and sensible training.

Volume I is also dedicated to the memory of former Nassau Community College Lions shooting guard, teammate, and friend Nathaniel Thomas.

# BASKETBALL STRENGTH TESTIMONIALS

"As a professional basketball player, I wanted to train different this summer, and not just lift weights the way I normally do. That's when a good friend of mine Dave showed me his system of functional training for basketball. I began doing things that I never thought I would be doing. Every workout was intense, and he pushes you to be physically and mentally strong. After doing these workouts I definitely feel stronger, I know I can handle anything mentally and physically. I translate these workouts on to the basketball court and it gives me that much more explosiveness in my game. I recommend this workout to anybody who is serious about Basketball and Staying in Basketball Shape".

**Mo Bailey**
**Professional Basketball Player**

"This is the most intense, sensible training I've ever experienced. It pushed me to my limits, making me a better conditioned athlete. I felt stronger and more explosive on the basketball court. No other workout can compare."

**Bryan Bailey**
**Professional Basketball Player**

# CONTENTS

"No door remains forever locked against the man of indomitable will and courage".

—Percy Wells Cerutty

# INTRODUCTION

Welcome to Basketball Strength – Volume I, my name is David Lemanczyk. I produced this system of functional Training to develop the minds and bodies of basketball players across the planet. This safe, sensible, natural, and progressive training course is for YOU, the aspiring player! I know that Professional Grade basketball players need to be in prime physical condition, to perform on a high level. I know that you understand that as well. Preparation is critical for future success. To develop and maintain this body, specific details need to be attended to which include but are not limited to dynamic stretching, physical conditioning, skill specific training and breathing exercises. You need the total package! Now, you have the keys to the total package in your possession. To be a true baller, you have to have it all. We move a specific way on the basketball court therefore we will work hard to develop that. To maximize our training and have it make sense, we need to perfect bodily movement and coordination which leads to optimal flexibility. Volume I is based on improving YOUR physical movement with safe exercises leading you to a path of physical independence.

At left, I am playing defense in a professional basketball game. I prided myself on playing tough defense because I took that aspect of the game personally. In terms of athletic preparation, I know what it takes to prepare your mind and body for a high level of play. Volume I in its entirety is the system I used to improve my physicality for the basketball court. Now you have that advantage too! (Photo by Joao Freitas)

# VOLUME I

This first installment of Basketball Strength is Volume I. The exercises within this training course represent the apex of basketball training. I have implemented every conceivable method of training for basketball and nothing compares to this. Ordinarily, coaches and strength professionals look to utilize basic weight training exercises for basketball players. This is definitely a step in the right direction however the player needs to develop optimal flexibility prior to that weight training. In short, develop flexibility first and build upon it. This is the most crucial step in physical training for improvement. If you skip this step, you will never reach your potential. Reach optimal flexibility! This Volume I system is metabolic conditioning. Metabolic conditioning applies to any type of sensible training that is carried on for long extended periods of time while promoting the highest levels of exercise integrity. Another premise behind metabolic training is that you will be stronger for longer and improve your entire body synergistically. You will not be working for twenty seconds at a time with breaks as long as five minutes between exercises. Instead, you will be expected to challenge yourself and push yourself for as long as you can.

As you get into the "doing" of this conditioning system you will note that each task and progression allows you to move exactly how you need to be moving to improve on the court. The intensity and fatigue you feel at the end of a game is exactly what you will feel like with the Volume I exercise. This is because I know you need to condition your body to be able to function positively during moments of tremendous fatigue. You need to be the player that is stronger for longer. You need to be the player that will not fatigue and can execute during moments of extreme pressure. The game of basketball is simple and can be complex due to poor physically and mentally development. Consider this training course as your overall ticket to learning and improving all aspects of yourself.

# SWAMP LUNGES

Any weak link in physicality or mentality will leak out onto the basketball court. As a successful athlete I know that is not acceptable. The only thing I will accept is success. As stated previously, Volume I will give you all the ammo you need to move like a baller. Make it happen right now, keep reading, and work to the big-time. Right out of the gate you must believe in the swamp lunge. In short; training starts and ends with the implementation of the swamp lunge. This movement will add to the improvement of your flexibility, conditioning and strength through diagonal traveling patterns. This exercise and its corresponding progressions represent a gold medal training system. This movement is the staple of my lower body training as well as the athletes I work with this proper and consistent practice represents the inevitable mastery within the physical body.

## SWAMP LUNGE EXECUTION

The execution of the swamp lunge is a smooth diagonal traveling movement. You want to treat learning this movement like learning how to walk for the first time, very carefully. You will no longer walk rather lunge diagonally. Take your time; allow your limbs to flow in their specific patterns. Smoothly go about every move and develop a rhythm.

1. Lift one knee high
2. Extend leg to outside diagonal
3. Absorb the force of the ground softly
4. Allow the back foot to turn and pivot

5.  Allow body to naturally come forward
6.  Push off your front heel to continue.
7.  Bring the back foot forward
8.  Lift that knee high & repeat process.

At left, the midpoint of a long stride swamp lunge (#5). Notice the necessary hip, glutei & hamstring flexibility. (Photo by Joan Lemanczyk)

The lunge itself is of a consistent diagonal nature. Convince yourself that you can only travel through this movement pattern. Allow your body to flow smoothly with this. Looking back at a traditional lunge, an athlete will lunge forward onto one foot for stabilization. Then the athlete will push off that front foot and return to the original starting position. This is good practice for standing in one specific place at all times. This is not the case here ladies and gentlemen. The swamp lunge is a functional task that brings optimal flexibility to the table immediately. Optimal simply means, a perfect amount. Attaining optimal flexibility should be your primary concern if you want to build a physical body. Without it, you can never receive full use of your bodily leverages. As stated previously, the swamp lunge requires an athlete to lunge in a diagonal "zigzag" type formation. The athlete's goal is to lunge to a diagonal position (45 degrees) consistently, with perfect form until momentary muscular failure. As most basketball players fatigue with this task it is most important to remember to; plant your foot on the ground then slowly and smoothly allow a deep stretch to consume the hips, gluteus, and hamstrings. Do not drop into a swamp lunge rather flow into it.

I have had success prompting athletes to lightly tap their knee to the ground to ensure OPTIMAL FLEXIBILITY. In the beginning this will only happen with short strides. A beginner should never attempt long strides with the slight knee tap on a soft surface. Remember to begin with the short stride and allow your body to develop correctly. This exercise is not intended for rush usage rather sensible progression.

At left, Bryan and Maurice Bailey demonstrate proper execution of the short stride swamp lunge, on grass. The benefits of training on soft natural surfaces such as grass will be detailed later in this Volume. Both Professional Basketball Players are using power bags held in bear hug position. This constant bear hug work increases upper body conditioning dramatically. I can surely tell you that neither of these guys is having a ball taken away from them. This represents a Phase II application. (Photo by Matt Lemanczyk)

It is also imperative to know that this knee tapping only occurs when you train on grass. I would advise you to train on grass as well because the surface is natural. Natural surfaces allow your body to develop without the unnecessary shock value of unnatural surfaces. If you do not have grass available, do not touch your knee to the ground (especially important).

## LOWER BODY MASTERY

When it comes down to improving the lower body, you must be serious. Let's face it, most people think of training and they think about upper-body improvement. Even better, most people think about improvement of those body parts that can be seen. This visual appeal improvement basis is often misleading and can lead to major muscular imbalances that can result in bodily harm. As stated previously, you need the total package. Your goal is balance and full function within your body. If you are reading this, you desire the total package. You have a deep understanding of your physical body and its need to be entirely efficient. There can be no weak links and if there are, they must improve immediately. I know you are serious about total body training. I know you have realized that total body conditioning unlocks the potential throughout the entirety of your body. The most impressive physical human beings on the planet possess extremely functional bodies. By functional, I simply mean flexible, durable, strong, powerful and injury resistant. That is what this Basketball Strength Volume I can provide you with, in time and with patience!

The swamp lunge and the execution I have described IS the essence of lower body development. It is a specific form of movement that allows you to fully develop naturally through leverage principles. You need to perform it correctly and develop a skill at it. There is no other lower body exercise that can produce what this exercise can, if performed correctly. I have attempted thousands of exercises and variations. Truth be told, many work but just not as well. This is why I used and continue to use it in my own training and for anyone I care about. I have improved athletes by the hundreds in the last six years. I owe a lot of the progress to my implementation of this dynamic task, its variations, and its progressions. It is important to know that the swamp lunge is as easy as "doing it" & "doing" is what will allow you to become skilled. Always remember that in anything you must be educated on what it is you are doing and why you are doing it. This information is available to all of you right now and in a format that can be understood. A teacher is only as good as his/her instruction.

The progressions in this professional grade product are outstanding and more importantly MAKE SENSE! When you take my advice and run this system you WILL make serous progress in your body. You will learn a lot about yourself with each workout. You will begin with the bodyweight swamp lunges I have already imposed upon all of you guys. Once you are able to begin using the power bags with the swamp lunges, your whole entire body gets into the mix, through natural movement.

## SWAMP LUNGE PROGRESSIONS

In the coming pages, I have listed a series of progressions to follow for basketball players. It is important to have all players follow the progressions exactly as they are written. Remember that once optimal flexibility is achieved then resistance can be added. You will know optimal flexibility when you see it by a basketball player demonstrating a stride that cannot be lengthened. This will be a different stride length for each player since each player is built differently. As stated previously once a stride length cannot be lengthened, optimal flexibility has been achieved. This means whoever this person is, they will be able to extract the most from their leverages. Look out time!

## SWAMP LUNGE MINDSET

A slow and steady mindset must be followed to achieve proper results. A basketball player must take this exercise and its variations slowly. If it helps you, think of the fluidity of an ocean breeze, all things smooth. Allow the body time to perfect each movement and do not rush through any progression. The stride length is going to be a direct indicator of the flexibility possessed by a basketball player (as described above). You will not force any movement because you flow smoothly into the movement. There is a flow involved that must be adhered to; mastery. The longer the players strides are, the more strength will be built throughout the entire lower body. You will dedicate yourself to lengthening your strides naturally. You will do this by being patient with own natural progress and in turn you will become more flexible in time. You will also be able to maximize those increased leverages on the basketball court immediately. This will enable you to increase your speed, acceleration and explosive ability on the basketball court. By now, it should become fairly obvious that you will obtain incredible results through this functional exercise if you perform in properly. Basketball players understand that their motor movement during a game is often unpredictable and intelligent coaches need to prepare them for that. Diagonal movements (swamp lunge for example) are used more often than any other form of movement in the game of basketball. This is why basketball players should option for the swamp lunge as opposed to the squat for their primary strength and conditioning movement. Think about the actual motor patterns basketball players must endure during a game whether it is offensively or defensively; always diagonals and explosive.

## THE CLOCK METHOD

In explaining the swamp lunge to athletes (which I love to do), I have produced a simple method. Before the digital age of wristwatches, there were watches made with two levers. One lever would regulate hours (short lever) and the other lever would regulate the minutes (long lever). Besides the levers, there were twelve numbers which represented hours. These numbers were read on the wristwatch in a "clockwise" fashion which simply translates into a circular rotation from right to left. Why am I mentioning the old-fashioned wristwatch? The old-fashioned wristwatch represents something most of us know and are familiar with. Therefore no matter what the task is, the explanation is taken with confidence. Any coach who is reading this book should use this simple association to drill the swamp lunge into your player's minds. It is important that the execution be correct the first time! Depending on an athlete's level of flexibility, the swamp lunge is going to vary in its execution. Obviously if optimal flexibility has not yet been reached the athlete will not be able to perform the exercise in its advanced stages, which are detailed in this book. A basketball player should always begin with a short stride during the swamp lunge and with their bodyweight as resistance. This exercise and its infinite variations are over a distance course until the form is lost. There can be NO mistakes and there is no other way around this cardinal rule. Once again, have your athlete's begin with short strides and week by week to SLOWLY lengthen the strides by inches. A one inch stride lengthen will make all the difference in the world. It places tremendous stress on the connective and soft tissues within the lower body.

At left, Bryan & Maurice Bailey are slowly raising their front thighs to ascend into the outward diagonal to complete Phase II of the swamp lunge. A soft, smooth application has to be the focus of swamp lunge execution. Both Bryan & Maurice keep a pace that suites their needs. They both understand how far to push themselves. (Photo by Matt Lemanczyk)

Traditionally and before I concentrated on it, I have had average flexibility throughout my body. Average flexibility to me is simply defined as; I could become more flexible through dynamic stretching but I was not exactly inflexible by any means. The implementation of the swamp lunge had enabled me to develop optimal flexibility throughout my lower body and become a tremendous basketball player at the same time. This was the KEY for me becoming a flexible, injury resilient, conditioned basketball player and a KEY member of the teams I played for. I began using short strides that were approximately two feet long in my experimentation of the swamp lunge. I understood the execution and the breathing coordination necessary to perform the task correctly. I spent a lot of time developing smooth, fluid strides that appeared effortless until momentary muscular failure. This work proved to be the foundation of unlocking my true potential. The point at which I achieved optimal flexibility is when my stride lengths were measured at a little over four and a half feet per. This did not happen overnight and was a result of sensible work. In terms of the stride length increase, I simply could not stride any longer. This is the point of optimal flexibility and an achievement reached. When you reach optimal flexibility, things begin to get interesting for you. I recommend distance courses and small challenges on a bi-weekly basis. Start yourself off with a hundred yards, then two, then three, etc.… I have and always will be a big believer in quality over quantity. Take one key note here; it is not specifically what you do that matters but HOW YOU DO IT! Make sure everything you perform in regards to basketball is correct. Basketball players need to train at the highest level in order to receive an apex of performance on the court. A fundamentally sound basketball player with tremendous strength and conditioning will not be beaten by anyone but him/herself. This system of training will make you feel like its crunch time in a game.

At left, I can be seen taking a jump shot during a game at the University of Bridgeport. I know a basketball player needs to shoot straight in order make shots consistently. Doing the same thing every time will allow you to make shots. This means daily practice of proper fundamentals in shooting straight at least two hundred makes. I advise that a player should develop his off two dribbles or less jump shot accompanying his catch and shoot ability. A player should also focus on footwork; jump stop, hop step and stride stop with a basketball. Properly implementing all three of the shooting footwork techniques allows basketball players to harness a complete arsenal. (Photo by Matt Lemanczyk)

# BALL HANDLING

Above, you can see me effectively handling a basketball. In specific, I have used my left hand to swing the ball around my back to my right hand. My body serves to shield the basketball from any defender. I utilize this around the back dribble anytime I need to. Once you develop the around the back dribble you have a safety valve for all possible pressures that you could face during ball handling. The practice of the Webster/Maravich drills helped to build the foundation of my ball handling ability. The stationary ball handling drills should always be mastered before progressing to the moving drills. You must give yourself a foundation of which to succeed and then build upon. You want the ball to feel like a yo-yo in your hand. (Photo by Joan Lemanczyk)

## DEFENSIVE STANCE

At left, you can see me executing a deep defensive stance with my hands in ready position. It is always important to keep the hands facing in front of you for protection. Practicing this stance along with the swamp lunge progressions will give you the endurance you need to keep your hands ready all the time. Having your hands down at your sides will not improve your playing ability. You need to practice this stance consistently during conditioning. (Photo by Joan Lemanczyk)

## WILL

The lactate threshold is a standard measurement based on the amount of lactic acid your body creates during extreme physical exercise (swamp lunges for example). This is referred to as the "burning sensation" felt during exercise. When the burning sensation proves too great for bodily function, momentary muscular failure is eminent. It is that specific point in time that you are finished with swamp lunges for that particular session. In the foundation of your training, you need to implement this one and done style. Your body will grow with you this way instead of you against your body. The level of conditioning that you can build is indescribable, you will see. Basketball players understand the game of basketball is fast paced with high energy. On the same token, basketball players and coaches should expect to work as hard as possible through the swamp lunge to achieve results. Does this sound any different than a well-designed play? All basketball players must execute this task with high efficiency just like an out of bounds play to win a game. Lemanczyk Rule # 1 = FINISH!

# SQUATS & SWAMP LUNGES

The squat exercise is one that ALL basketball coaches had depended upon for the lower body during the time (1996-1997) I had been attending Junior College. I agreed that the squat is an outstanding exercise but ball players in any sport do not need to perform them to play at a high level. I do NOT agree that basketball players should begin their training with them for increased on-court performance for one main reason: lack of overall optimal flexibility. You cannot build a foundation on unstable ground. I knew then that there was something more functional that could benefit me than the popular squat exercise. I also understood that I needed to play well to receive a basketball scholarship to attend a four-year University post Junior College. I needed to prepare my body by doing something specific to succeed on the basketball court in training. The squat just did not cut it! How can any basketball player squat BEFORE achieving optimal flexibility in a conditioning program? How can any basketball player expect to improve as an athlete without optimal flexibility? A basketball player should NOT squat until he/she has developed the optimal flexibility of the lower body. The realistic option and recipe for success in developing this is through the implementation of the swamp lunge. Once optimal flexibility is achieved the squat, or any other exercise can be safely implemented. Let us face it, real ball players need to be flexible ALL THE TIME. Flexible joints with optimal ranges of movement give basketball players high resilience towards injury. Exercises like the swamp lunge performed correctly enable this flexibility to happen. The swamp lunge is a dynamic stretch that I turned into functional application for YOU! Every basketball player can expect to gain from hard training with this functional method. This is a necessity for the high profile player that cares deeply for the body. Dynamic stretches are demonstrated through smooth fluid motions like the swamp lunge for example. Static stretches are smooth stretches and held in position for extended time periods utilizing lung power techniques. These stretches are to be performed at the VERY END of any activity where blood flow and increased circulation has been attained. Take each stretch slow, feel it out, and cease the motion when you feel necessary. Everything is smooth.

## ADEQUATE BODY CARE

A true ballers program is simple and hard. On off-training days, ballers must jump rope/jumping jacks (upon rising) then soak their bodies in contrast baths. Contrast baths are warm and cold water baths for extended time periods of thirty minutes or more. I recommend thirty minutes cold and thirty minutes warm thereafter. Make the time for this because it works. One hour per day submerged in water will do wonders for the body. I call the effects, "flotion." Simply sit, relax, and read. "Flotion" is an understanding of gravity, water, and its effect on the human body. Submerging the body fully into water can force internal bodily process to work in a slightly different manner. For example, breathing becomes essential and more highlighted. The weightless environment is quite a change! This is due to the lack of gravity within the water environment. The "shock" value of movement is completely eliminated. Extended contrast baths or "flotion" is when bodily process can heal soft tissues the quickest. There is no constant shock absorption as that of traveling on the Earth's surface. This allows joints to heal because the human body can heal itself to a remarkably high degree, if given the opportunity and the time. The body operates to heal. The understanding of how to allow your body to work in this manner is the path to true physical mastery. Breathing exercises during "flotion" baths pay huge dividends. Your body must experience sunlight daily for at least an hour. You will use sun block because there are no trophies for sunburns.

I also recommend a daily wake up before dawn for deep breathing exercises. Building lung power is another key to building the foundation that is your physical body. The usage of air for depression and the imposition of force are undeniable. Once developed, lung power is used for anything human body related. Our bodies operate with a consistent flow of breathable air. Without the air we breathe, we are like fish out of water with little time left. Your entire body will improve its function by your application of lung power exercises. Breathing is a process that occurs in the following fashion: in through the nose and out of the mouth. Your nutrition should be consistent with natural foods such as fruits, vegetables, grains, nuts, and water. You do not need to add salt to your meals because your body naturally makes its own. You do not need to add sugar either as any sugar you ingest should come naturally within fruits. You need daily exposure to sunlight and fresh, clean air. You should eat and drink when you need to and not when you want to. There is a human instinct to eat when hungry, drink when thirsty and sleep when tired. This is something that you should obey if physical progress is what you want. Anything processed will take longer for your body to break down use for energy. In most cases, these packaged foods lead to the most common colds when consumed too often. The reason is the compounds cannot be digested in your system at a rate of which you consume. Treat your body with what it needs as opposed to what you want to have. Anything else is irrational and we know that.

At the beginning or end of a workout I really enjoy spinning the basketball on my fingers (see picture left). I actually use this as a hand, finger and wrist warm up when I play basketball. The ability to spin on the ball on all your fingers will give you added dexterity. That increased tangible will provide you with a more functional pair of hands. I also recommend you take the basketball and slap it with both of your hands until warm. You need to develop the force absorption qualities in your lower arms for game preparation.

# BASKETBALL CONDITIONING

By now, you already know how strongly I feel about proper instruction for basketball players. I mean, you really have to simulate specific things in order to achieve specific results. For example; let's say your goal as the player is to improve your defense. As a pertinent coach, I am going to teach you how to improve and effectively condition yourself to move in that specific fashion. This makes obvious sense. Basketball conditioning applies to methods of training that truly prepare the player for competition. You won't find anything in this actual course that is unnecessary. The course and its progressions make sense. You do not need to be able to lift a lot of weight to improve as a basketball player. You need to play basketball and condition yourself properly. You can achieve that level of physicality by using this course for your conditioning. Volume I represents true, attainable methods of physical training. It all begins with the constant diagonal movement in swamp lunge training. We personally know that this movement prepares a player for diagonal movement. Diagonal movement is the movement most often used in the game and in any bipedal life moment. Any time a player cuts, fakes, drives, passes, moves, he/she will use a step to a diagonal at some point. This diagonal move is the maker or breaker of a true offensive player. Imagine yourself with the basketball and you're standing just outside the three point arc. You take the ball from triple threat position and sweep left. You allow the momentum from your powerful sweep to carry you to the left diagonal. It is at this specific point in time that the swamp lunge proves most crucial. When you need your body to serve you functionally in the toughest spots, it must; that is the bottom line.

Swamp lunge implementation allows you to be able to depend on both legs for stability. Your training will allow you to learn this about yourself and feel the improvements as they are made in time. It has been a catch phrase of recent academic times to mention the following; stability creates mobility. This physical training does not take the place of your actual basketball skill work. This conditioning is necessary for you to improve ALONG with your skill work. You still need to practice your ball handling, passing, shooting, defending and 1 on 1 moves daily. The conditioned player can expect to use this system of training once every three days. That means in between that time, you STILL practice your individual skills daily. This point is essential. Daily skill work also serves as a consistent flow of cardiovascular exercise. Cardiovascular exercise allows the body to increase its blood flow over an extended period of time and promote healing. You do this every day. I have been told that my swamp lunge instruction reminds people of learning a martial arts movement. My response has and always will be; basketball is a martial art. The movements, there fluidity reminds me of the arts. Come to think of it, I have heard somewhere that Strength & Conditioning Coach Kim Wood mentioned that as well. He is one of the most sensible men on the planet in terms of physicality. Basketball players are required to perform every loco motor form of movement during competition not to mention explosive manipulative ball skills and the prerequisite peripheral vision required to play at a high level. You can prepare yourself for game time by going through with this physical training. Through it you will learn that something valuable about yourself. It is amazing that something so simple can be so incredibly effective. Once that realization comes through for you, you will have already made obvious progress.

## TODAY & TOMORROW

Athletic events that occur yesterday, today, and tomorrow are the ones we seem to remember most. I think about my last game because it is what I have just done. I am prepared to improve upon my last performance TODAY because I need to. We will worry about tomorrow when it comes. This is the mindset right here. You can control your destiny because you are going to prepare to succeed. This is a realistic plan proven repeatedly with the cost of your time and effort. Concentrating on the events we can control will create positive opportunities for us. We can dedicate ourselves to the fundamental skills of the game and physical conditioning. If you are in shape and skilled in the fundamentals nobody can stop you. From this point it is all about mental toughness. How much can you take, how far are you willing to go, and how bad do you want it? Use the positive information in Volume I to shut off all negative thoughts coming from your mind (quitting before the form is lost). You will take control of your mind and be the dominator of your own body. You must learn when you are your body truly fails and not your mind's eye. You will be finished with an exercise when you are truly physically finished not when you think you are. You will learn to feel and know when you are done. If you learn your true failure moments in time you can prepare your will to combat, it sensibly. Once you understand and dominate your will versus failure, your potential will be in reach in time. It is a fact that the mind can and will control the body if you develop the necessary cognitive strength. Some people also call this mental toughness, and this is something I know to be true. Great basketball players have extreme levels of mental toughness because they do not know how to give up. They will not give up and do not know how to give anything less than a full effort all the time! The barrier that separates champion athletes from athletes is the invisible line of will versus pain. Imagine for a second that you are a basketball coach. Your team has fifteen players. Imagine any team conditioning drill (seventeen's for example) and which athlete can you see lasting the longest? Who will be the last man standing? I can tell you the man that lasts longest holds two major attributes. One is that he has the finest cardiovascular fitness for the exercise. Secondly, he might be the most mentally tough (will). Put the two together and you have a chance at a big-time player. Any cardiovascular activity under high intensity brings out the overall truth in an athlete. You will know where the level of physical conditioning and mental toughness are immediately. "Break down city" is a name I like to use to describe the process. Everyone will break down and that is a reality. If performed the proper way, a break down can be your body's form of compliment. The athlete will realize and believe in the ability to come back strong. This is where the commitment really becomes prevalent. Those afraid of the pain will draw the line and stop here. Those who understand and grasp the concept will make phenomenal progress. Everything else that follows from this point on represents success. Building mental toughness can occur over time if the athlete is willing to learn from experience. This requires a personal commitment to conditioning. This is called a "sacrifice" because of the reckless abandon that is publicly witnessed in training. The athlete must also simply understand the difference between pain and injury to gain versus loss. To understand pain and injury is to understand loss. In order to not experience any negative outcomes or loss, you need to learn how much you are capable of. Take the swamp lunges for example; do them correctly when of course your fitness level is in accordance with the distance task. When your form fails, the exercise is done for that day with that exercise.

## DEVELOPING CONFIDENCE

Beyond the obvious factor of pain, confidence separates athletes. Confidence enables an athlete to carry out a specific task when it is required. Confidence provides a sense of positive well-being in the mind of an athlete. For example, anyone who shoots a basketball should expect to make every single shot. If not, pass the ball. To develop this confidence in oneself, proper skill and physical training is necessary. Confidence comes with proper repetition and success in training. No matter what sport the athlete is in, skill specific work is to be completed daily. As stated previously, cardiovascular fitness is to be exhibited daily. Applied functional training every three days (off-season) and once a week (in-season). The rigors and demands of in-season athletics require a maintenance application of sensible physical training. This is a smart way used by successful athletes over the years.

## CONFIDENCE VERSUS ARROGANCE

Depending on whom you talk to confidence and arrogance can be perceived through different eyes. You could have two noticeably confident people who are viewed as arrogant by outside individuals. The same could be said for arrogant people. How do you know the difference? Confidence is an ability to understand one's personal capabilities. This is a deep understanding of oneself. This is an all-powerful knowing of what a person is capable of. How can a person know what they are capable of if they have never attempted to achieve beyond known expectations? You cannot. It is time to overachieve. Arrogance is a person once confident, now complacent. Once an accomplishment is earned, the arrogant person must harp on it. They must milk the cow of accomplishment for all it is worth. The arduous work ceases for the joy, thrill and pats on the back of previous accomplishments. This is an example of achieving but most importantly NOT reaching potential. Confidence is an ally and arrogance are an enemy. All athletes need to remain confident to succeed. Sports are games measured by statistics. The statistics are measured in regard to failure versus success rates. Since most sports are failure orientated (pessimistic point of view), confidence in athletes must remain high for success to be consistent. If an athlete is not confident, then how could he/she remain consistently successful? They cannot. Athletes must always be confident for success and overachievement. The game of life is no different. The same principles apply. Statistics measure everything according to success and failure. It all comes down to confidence and arrogance since athletes are the ones participating. Confidence leads to overachieving and arrogance leads to underachieving. Complacent is a dictionary word that a confident and successful person understands because that is never an option. It is a recipe for disaster, leads to personal character danger and underachieving. The arrogant person disregards the same word because it requires that they point the finger inward at them self. This means self-reflection. Arrogance is ugly therefore it is ignored if temporary success is achieved. An arrogant person will not look in the mirror to see the truth. Only what is on the surface. Sometimes the arrogant person wins the battle, but the confident person always wins the war. Time and patience bring out all the answers. Athletes need confidence to overachieve.

## MAXIMIZING YOUR ABILITY

If you want to learn how to maximize your natural abilities on the hardwood, continue reading. This next installment includes pivotal information for ballers everywhere. The swamp lunge is the key for our offensive movement. Let that become a staple in your mind once again as a reminder of how ballers should move. So much work goes into physical conditioning that sometimes the basic skills of the game are cast aside. This is obviously backwards as skill specific work should always dominate an athlete's workload and then physical conditioning. If you are smart, you will then combine the two. Once you have done that you will achieve Basketball Strength. Each athlete has his own personal level of physical and mental talents. If the man is smart, he will understand how to apply his talents to the game he plays. Take a physically talented basketball player for example. This basketball player understands how to maximize his ability on the court. He understands his capabilities because he has developed them through consistent drilling. His body is no secret, and he knows where he resides in time and space. All those talents are tremendous to hold but wielding them in the most correct fashion is the challenge. The fact is that there is a plethora of physically talented players. There is NOT however an equal number of mentally or cognitively talented players. This is improved through dedicated focus in training. Sometimes it is not how high you jump but how you can implement that skill within the parameters of the team's goals. Once you have ability, you need to understand it. Basketball strength is a thinking basketball player's tool. Use it to maximize your ability and potential right now! You have the power to improve when you use this system. Read and become these words to improve.

## MAXIMIZING YOUR LEVERAGE

The human body is comprised of multiple levers (bones & joints) with several different properties. Each joint has a specific movement attached to it. Hinge joints (knee) only move through flexion and extension. Ball and socket joints (shoulder) can rotate and move in multiple directions with range of motion depending on the individual's flexibility. Learn how your body can move and improve it naturally, smoothly. The concept of leverage is basic in its nature yet is seems to evade the minds of the average trainee/player. In basketball, the concept of leverage can easily decide a winner from a loser. Whoever reaches the *leverage vantage point* will be the athlete who takes home the gold trophy. Leverage can be gained by simply reading your opponent and executing. You want to look at the positioning of your opponent's levers (body positioning) and exploit it. Basketball is a leverage game. Can you achieve a lower position than your competitor and drive through to accomplish your goal of establishing position? Yes, you can, and you will. These are the questions you will ask yourself. This is what you are supposed to be looking for when you are on the court.

The name of the game is positioning and only through leverage is this possible. You must understand that an optimally flexible athlete is a more efficient athlete since imposed maximum leverage on an opponent is more likely to be reached. This athlete can use the maximum of his ability and impose his will. Basketball players need discipline, mental toughness, and dedication to ensure constant improvement. Knowing how the body works in relation to time and space elevates a player's game. This is taught and learned through repetitions of game-like movements and cardiovascular exercise; chalk one up for conditioning. When you know your body the game of basketball becomes easier. Taking what a defense gives is an effective scoring strategy. Taking an offensive standpoint is also an effective scoring strategy. The offense needs development to be effective. Once that is acquired and disposed your opponents will be forced to play the "hope you miss" defense.

## OVERACHIEVEMENT

In my basketball career, I have persevered and worked my way from the lowest levels of basketball to the highest in the world. My travels in the game of basketball took me from the parks of New York, the scholastic (High School) level through to the Junior College level, the University level, and finally the Professional Basketball level. I have had the opportunities to learn from a variety of outstanding coaches and mentors through my athletics career. I attribute my personal success on the basketball court to overachievement and the help of my past teammates, coaches and opponents. I always knew I would become a professional basketball player as long as I worked hard, kept my ears open and my mouth shut. That is a great lesson for many players.

## PREPARE TO SUCCEED

Reaching your potential as a basketball player requires a commitment to the fundamental skills of the game. You are also required to obey your coach, the system he/she implores and most importantly yourself as an individual person. This is a growing experience and something that will stay with you for the rest of your life. You must take each training day as a gift because you are lucky to be able to participate in the greatest sport of all time. Remember to be thankful for the people that show you the way to reaching your potential as an adult and as a basketball player. In time, you will give back. You will learn a lot about yourself mentally and physically through the trial and error involved in Basketball Strength. You are on your way to becoming the finest basketball player you can possibly be. Preparation is everything when it comes to molding a basketball player and I am happy to show you how right now!

## COMMITMENT

Basketball players NEED to have personal commitment to reach a prominent level of conditioning for game time purposes. Basketball players must become strong, durable, and ready for all situations basketball and never run out of gas! Make the commitment to yourself now and prepare to succeed! The difference between someone that trains and one that goes through the motions is simply gut-wrenching efforts. When your mind tells you to quit you cannot quit. A lot of people do, and their training results directly reflect that. You must completely dedicate yourself to training because you understand smart, hard work yields positive results. Allow your body to decide for itself and learn the cautionary signs of muscular failure. This is true physical learning. The first time a basketball player runs this system, he/she is incredibly surprised of the outcome. The experience is tougher than expected because a perfect execution effort is expected for success. Developing perfect strides through the swamp lunge will allow your body to move that way it was intended to.

## FULL RANGES OF MOTION

Range of motion training is simple, yet highly effective. This method revolves around using the human body for what it was made to do. If you feel around your body, you will notice that your joints are set up on angles. These angles create and differentiate leverage points. Joints usually work across two planes as well. To train a range of motion is to develop a full range of motion first. Once a full range of motion is developed it must be trained from all angles. Developing joints through multi angle movements are exactly what a physical body need. You can do swamp lunges for the rest of your life; never add any resistance and you will achieve an insurmountable level of fitness. Tiny amounts of resistance are to be added. This weighted resistance must be added in form of functional training and with a progressive overload principle in mind. Time, patience and little by little philosophies work. The functional training I speak of is simple. In short; train for life and NOT for the mirror. If you do this, your body will work when you need it to.

For example; swamp lunges in anyone's training program regardless of physical activity is highly effective. This is because all ranges of motion within the entire lower body are worked in their natural forms. The swamp lunge should become a natural movement like walking; efficiency is your goal. It will be mentioned one last time that the joints range of motion must be full before any resistance is added. Keep this rule embedded in your mind and it will help you. When you train a joints full range of motion intelligently, you will strengthen its overall properties. Connective and soft tissues (muscles) are conditioned to be used for future function. The bones that support the joints are also strengthened. This greatly reduces any chance of injury and serves as a preventative method for injury. Athletes need to be healthy to participate and not dissipate on the sidelines. If the burning sensation is too great and you lose form, you are now susceptible to injury. You MUST cease the exercise when your form breaks down. I want EVERYTHING you do to be with good form in mind. This keeps you safe and positive.

## MENTAL TOUGHNESS IN TRAINING = GAME TOUGHNESS

During the swamp lunge the human body (mind included) is searching for a way to recruit every muscle fiber for task completion. This is the body's natural reaction to put a clamp on the pain (lactate threshold). How many times have you witnessed a basketball player play intense defense for twenty seconds consecutively and have his opponent score on him due to lack of endurance? Basketball players who commit themselves to excellence are the players who succeed overall. You do this and you will overachieve. Basketball players need to have tremendously durable bodies, beginning primarily with their lower bodies. Hardnosed basketball players and coaches know that you do not quit on anything when you know you can be successful. As previously stated, when performing the swamp lunge, if the burning sensation (lactate threshold) is too great and you are losing form, you are DONE! As a general rule, this exercise will end once your form is lost. If you do not follow that cardinal rule of the swamp lunge you will become susceptible to sports injury. Once again, once the form is lost you MUST cease the exercise. I want ALL SWAMP LUNGES you perform to be with good form in mind because we need to maximize your leverages to carry onto to the court.

## FREQUENCY & INTENSITY

A simple guideline regarding training frequency for the Basketball Strength Volume I and accompanying exercises is as follows; train one day, rest the body, when it is no longer sore from exercise, train again. This is your training schedule, one day at a time. Remember to concentrate on developing the proper movements through each exercise. The following phases and progressions in this book have been pedagogically designed. This means there is common sense behind them and done so by a qualified instructor. My overall goal for you is to obtain and maintain a high level of fitness. I want this level to be so high that people, at time, will question your validity, your methods and you in general. When someone questions your validity, they are really comparing themselves to you and inwardly questioning their own development. When the comparison is not even close, people look to point fingers and these fingers will be soon at you. You have to be ready to accept greatness.

Another goal I have for you that I have stated previously is your path to overall independence in physical training. I am giving you movement patterns, specific exercises, and ways of which to condition the body. I am not interested in developing a method of ensuring a cosmetic look, but this type of training will yield the most obvious physical results. You will be in the best shape of your life when you run this system. Your energy levels will be at an all time high and so will your daily productivity no matter what you do. If you ever need a resource to remember how to properly care for the body, just look back in this book. Volume I is intended to be your sole physical training guide and has been formatted properly to answer sensible training questions.

The progressions inside this product work together with basic biomechanics in mind. Instead of the all too common nowadays approach where a coach uses a machine/gadget to have his players teach their bodies, I use a player's body to teach his body. The mind is the sole controller of the body therefore it must be properly conditioned with the correct motor and sensory progressions to ensure success. Basketball players are the most elite movers on the planet and should train specifically for that. I wish you all the best of health and strength. Work hard, never make an excuse and you will overachieve. Together we can become champions, the time is now yours.

To improve the vertical leap, look to develop the stride length in the entire lower body first. When you develop your leverages to an optimal range you can receive full use of them. This represents the path to optimal flexibility henceforth your physical potential. Once you develop your stride length to its optimal range, now it is time to work on full extension. In the picture above, you can see that I receive the maximum from my leverages. (Photo by Joan Lemanczyk)

# 15LB CANVAS POWERBAG
# SLAM DUNK

# PHASE I

## PHASE I, COURSE I

Swamp lunges with bodyweight resistance, using short stride length and with hands held in defensive stance. Hold your hands in proper defensive position as long as you can.

1. Hands held high and out to sides in defensive position for duration of lunge.
2. High knee and fully extend one leg to the diagonal.
3. Land on that heel to absorb body's force.
4. Turn and pivot back foot forwards on the ball of foot.
5. Allow body to lean forward into a full lunge smoothly.
6. Just before knee touches the court push off front heel only.
7. High knee and fully extend opposite leg to repeat process.

Repeat until form is lost. This is the first phase, so it is imperative that you get it right. Start out with slow, diagonal strides. When I work with an athlete, I use the cue of, "Stride to the side" to catch form attention. Everything must be smooth including the landing on the heel of the foot, and the back foot pivot for accommodation.

The short stride enables the quadriceps muscles of the legs to work hard. This is due to the angle the joints of the leg are in during this exercise. An athlete should look to develop this stride until everything is smooth. No part of this exercise should be a rush or a race at this point in your training. In a lot of ways, this training is like learning to walk.

Take it slow; make sure you raise the knee as high and smoothly with each stride. This is a major hip flexor and abdominal builder not to mention balance and stability. Keep in mind that Stability enables Mobility.

Work yourself up to only pushing off the front heel with each stride. You will see me demonstrate this in the DVD. When you start, you should use both feet to push yourself up. This would include your front heel and back ball of the foot. This is a type of lunging method that I refer to as a scissor lunge. Your goal is to short stride it pushing off your front heels only. This will develop tremendous stability within the knee.

This is the beginning of your new movement basis. Walking and moving this way is completely different from any other form of training. You will know what I mean once you get going with it. Work hard with this and be very smart.

**P.S.** Be patient and allow yourself to master this movement. This is an extremely critical learning moment in your physical development. Succeed here and reap rewards later!

## PHASE I, COURSE II

Swamp lunges with bodyweight resistance, using medium stride length and with hands held in defensive stance. Keep your hands UP! You need to develop your shoulder girdles conditioning to a point where you are strong for long. If your hands go down before your lunges are complete, swing them upward with each stride. You can also thrust your hands forward simulating a powerful shove. Be safe & creative.

1. Hands held high and out to sides in defensive position for duration of lunge.
2. High knee and fully extend one leg to the diagonal.
3. Land on heel to absorb body's force.
4. Turn and pivot back foot forwards on the ball of foot.
5. Allow body to lean forward into a full lunge smoothly.
6. Just before knee touches the court push off front heel only.
7. High knee and fully extend opposite leg to repeat process.

Repeat until form is lost. A medium stride is a profoundly serious point in swamp lunging. This stride increase is going to place more stress onto the hamstring than in the short stride. Remember, the short stride will place more of an emphasis onto the quadriceps. This again, is due to the angle of the joint and working muscles.

You should look to stay with this medium stride for at least a couple months. This is a dramatic difference from that of the short stride length. You will experience soreness like never before once you use a medium stride for distances exceeding one hundred yards.

Keep in mind that when your hands go down from shoulder girdle fatigue that a new game begins. Challenge yourself to use your arms in creative ways while you swamp lunge. Throw smooth, form palm strikes simultaneous with each stride. Throw both of your hands forward (pushing). The list is endless, but you should use those movements since they will hold importance to basketball players.

Push and pull your arms in all different directions. It is important for you to learn how you can move your body during actual movement. The integration of motor skills here is truly where your success will be determined. Work on lengthening, twisting, and moving through safe patterns of movement.

# PHASE I, COURSE III (OPTIMAL FLEXIBILITY)

Swamp lunges with bodyweight resistance, using long stride length and with hands held in defensive stance. At this point, you know what you need to do with your hands once they fall from shoulder girdle fatigue. In case you need a reminder; use them.

1. Hands held high and out to sides in defensive position for duration of lunge.
2. High knee and fully extend one leg to the diagonal.
3. Land on heel to absorb body's force.
4. Turn and pivot back foot forwards on the ball of foot.
5. Allow body to lean forward into a full lunge smoothly.
6. Just before knee touches the court push off front heel only.
7. High knee and fully extend opposite leg to repeat process.

The swamp lunge with a long stride length is no joke, especially when you're only pushing off the front heel. When you see someone performing them this way it will leave you with your mouth open. This is the point at which an athlete develops lower body optimal flexibility. This is the apex of flexibility and the foundation of which to build the absolute foundation. There will be a time of fantastic improvement and when a player truly can expect to reach apex in potential. An athlete can also expect to place tremendous emphasis onto the gluteus, hips, hamstrings and quadriceps muscles.

The shear flexibility in the hip joints needed for this long stride length is worth mentioning. You need to work VERY hard consistently to get to this point in training. Trust me when I say spend time on the short and medium stride lengths. It is mostly due to the time your connective tissues need for the proper adaptation to take place.

This long stride length recruits an athlete's entire system of muscles to complete the lever. The lever is strengthened each time you push off that front heel. Once you can swamp lunge using only the front heel for distance, you are a monster. Remember to keep your upper body moving and breathe!

Once I got to this point (long stride) in my training, I began swamp lunging for one hundred yards at a time. I would look to make the distance smoothly first. Then I would slowly improve my total elapsed time per one hundred yards. This training is for real and you will know it when you feel it. Imagine how a quarter mile swamp lunge feels?

As stated previously, once you have reached the long stride length, optimal flexibility is apparent. It is when you spend dedicated training sessions developing this long stride that will allow you to progress to the Powerbag realm.

Developing the long stride diagonal swamp lunge will give you a complete dominance over the way your body moves over the ground. You will know this when you feel it for yourself. Have confidence in your ability to succeed and make progress.

**P.S**. Vertical leaps are developed using dynamic movements, resting, and then feeding the body to increase recovery time. Make sure to make an emphasis on natural food selections and hydration when implementing this Basketball Strength program.

## PHASE I, COURSE IV (OPTIMAL FLEXIBILITY)

Swamp lunges with bodyweight resistance, using long stride length, with hands held in defensive stance & leaning forward over front knee. You DON'T need any other resistance other than yourself! This is when you learn how to use yourself for yourself.

1. Hands held high and out to sides in defensive position for duration of lunge.
2. High knee and fully extend one leg to the diagonal.
3. Land on heel to absorb body's force.
4. Turn and pivot back foot forwards on the ball of foot.
5. Allow body to lean forward over front knee into a full lunge smoothly.
6. Just before knee touches the court push off front heel only.
7. Use arms to generate momentum upwards as you fatigue.
8. High knee and fully extend opposite leg to repeat process.

Repeat until form is lost. This addition is simple and makes sense. Since our upper bodies hold weight, we should use our own body for the resistance. After you have landed on the front heel, smoothly lean your body over that knee. Your lower back will stretch dynamically, and your body will be able to naturally align it. Learn to flex and extend your back in synergy with your breathing/striding. At this point you should be able to push off the front heel solely. Once you do you will notice the difference in your knee strike. Coming out of a crouched lunge into a knee strike takes coordination. This is an aspect of swamp lunging that highly relates combat. Remember to keep everything smooth and develop your ranges of motion.

Keep the hands busy and challenge yourself. Think about the different movements your upper body will be asked to perform during a game. Perform one movement with each stride smoothly. This is a time when balance, coordination, and fitness is developed. Take a realistic challenge and see if you can perform this exercise variation for a one-hundred-yard distance. Make sure you breathe and use your upper body with each stride. Swing your arms upwards to help you generate momentum, push them forward, and row them backwards. You should also feel free to use movements you know happen within the game. The pushes, the quick stabs for deflections, closing and opening your hands are all important pieces to this process of improvement.

If you take the bodyweight distance challenge and put it to bed, you can definitely still train bodyweight only and expect to gain results. This is when you can begin slowly twisting your upper body with each stride. You do this because you can and will. I advise you perform your swamp lunges with palm strikes in smooth fashion. Allow your body to flow into each palm strike. This is a smooth, form addition to allow you to build an element of survival with basketball strength. It is important that a player understand how important this actually. Develop powerful palm strikes with each stride.

## ONE STRIDE, ONE BREATH, ONE PALM STRIKE

**P.S.** Doing swamp lunges with palm strikes are one of the fastest ways to total body fitness. Make sure your palm strikes are as smooth as each swamp lunge stride. Throw smooth palm strikes in all directions improving total ranges of motion within the entire body.

# PHASE I CHALLENGE

Good work with the first phase of the swamp lunge. Going through the short, medium, long stride length variations proves its weight in gold. You should already notice daily movement improvement along with relief of bodily pain and improved conditioning. When we talk conditioning we are really talking Metabolic Conditioning. As stated previously, this term applies to the athlete who decides he will work the smartest, hardest and most intense for as long as he possibly can while keeping integrity at its highest level. A Metabolic Conditioning application for you is the quarter mile swamp lunge. This IS the challenge for Phase I. Think about it, you have already swamp lunged hundreds of yards. One hundred, two hundred strides at a time and consistently. You ARE ready for the quarter mile challenge. Win each challenge and raise your bar! Go to a track, pick a lane and rock out. If you don't have a track, measure out one hundred and ten yards and do it four times. A quarter mile is four hundred and forty yards. This is going to be a test of your strength, endurance, wills, mental toughness and lung power. You will experience the lactate threshold in a whole new light. So go for yours and let me know how the experience changed your outlook on training. Will you ever need to perform any movements for your lower body? No. Do you need anything outside of yourself to put proper movement together? No. I came up with a series of stipulations for this challenge and I will list them below. This is how I challenge myself beyond the challenge itself. I do NOT recommend this for anyone else who has not attained a high level of fitness. This is a direct result of challenging me to ensure steady progress and fun in training.

- No raising hands over my head at any point.
- No stopping during the task, pausing only when needed.
- No leaning over, kneeling/resting.

When you can knock down a hundred yards without stopping in the long stride swamp lunge, you are achieving results. This type of endurance leads to personal challenges much like the quarter mile challenge. Now, the quarter mile challenge differs on the scale of difficulty. The execution is still the same.

A sensible approach to distance lunges would be to gradually increase strides per session. A general rule is that you can stride until your form breaks down. You will have to find the pace that works best for you. This pace is essentially a level that most people will not reach through general "go through the motions training".

Volume I metabolic conditioning allows basketball players to compete with the highest levels of their physicality. At left, you can see me finishing another one-handed hammer. I have always enjoyed the feeling of throwing it down; the rush when the ball is screaming through the net with my hand on the iron. (Photo by Joan Lemanczyk)

The triple threat offensive position is where everything begins when a player has the basketball. This position demonstrates dominance and confidence in ability. A player must use a forceful power sweep to move in any direction. This power sweep is developed through repetition using the basketball while starting a move. Above, you can see me in triple threat position about to power sweep right. (Photo by Joan Lemanczyk)

Before I even touch a basketball, I begin a series of self-imagery exercises. These cognitive/visualization training methods are normally used for five minutes before actual skills training. To begin, I walk around the basketball court and use slow motion loco motor movements that I normally use in a game. This includes imaginary, ball handling, shooting, the hop step, jump stop, and stride stop. As I go through the motions of the triple threat, offensive power sweep and one on one move, I can create a game-like "feel" in training. This type of mental preparation creates a positive foundation to build upon. Once your five minutes of self-visualization is completed, get to your skills drills. This helps clear the mind. (Photo by Joan Lemanczyk) Here is a real good individual workout to follow to increase skills.

- Maravich Drills (5 minutes)
- 1 Dribble Shooting/ 2 Dribble Shooting (10 minutes)
- Defensive Movement (5 minutes)
- Post Moves (10 minutes)
- Free Throw Conditioning/Shooting (10 minutes)
- Wall Passing (5 minutes)
- 17's (perform once all out to end it)

# ELEMENTAL TRAINING

Training outside close to nature has tremendous benefit for a basketball player. The fresh air and sunshine contains obvious naturopathic benefit. It is always important for a ball player to understand the very essence of nature and its relationship to us. I always advise training outside as opposed to congested and germ filled rooms. There are times when you will be limited to inside training. Until you are forced inside, get outside, and make it happen. Listening to birds and breathing free air is something that will immediately improve your training. The elements of air, wind and earth are hard at work, and you have the chance to use it to your advantage. At left, you can see me at my favorite park about to begin some serious Basketball Strength conditioning. (Photo by Joan Lemanczyk)

The time for you to begin this Basketball Strength conditioning is coming soon. This Volume I will give you the information you need to create your own path to physical independence. As you can see from the picture, the powerbags are off the ground and on top of my shoulders now. This represents my domination over them and the beginning of my physical improvement. An athlete should always succeed in his/her mind before any reality-based attempts on anything are made. Visualize your success and then become a part of it. At left, I am ready to begin my conditioning. Are you ready to begin yours? (Photo by Joan Lemanczyk)

# PHASE II

## PHASE II, COURSE I

Swamp lunges with bag in bear hug position using short stride length.

I advocate a no more than a fifteen-pound increase in weighted resistance for this exercise. You can progress safely to a weight of twenty-five pounds after you can complete the long stride for distances over one hundred yards consistently.

We now go back to the short stride length because added resistance other than our bodyweight represents tremendous stress on our lower body levers. Once you make the upgrade to using weighted resistance, you have really stepped it up. Simply repeat your perfected and smooth short stride form.

1. Bear hug bag tightly.
2. High knee and fully extend one leg to the diagonal.
3. Land on heel to absorb body's force.
4. Turn and pivot back foot forwards on the ball of foot.
5. Allow body to lean forward into a full lunge smoothly.
6. Just before knee touches the court push off front heel only.
7. Maintain erect back posture.
8. High knee and fully extend opposite leg to repeat process.

Repeat until form failure. This bear hug position will keep your upper body working consistently. The actual workload is one of absolute endurance and mental toughness. During your lunging you might believe that your arms are being trained as hard as or harder than your lower body.

Remember to squeeze and crush the resistance (sandbags, power bags, medicine ball) when they are held in your bear hug position. You must work intelligently in every possible way without making training difficult and ridiculous. There is never a reason to complicate physical training. Always keep it simple and stick to the basics of exercise integrity.

A military duffle bag and a fifty-pound bag of sand are the two things that go perfect for the rest of this training. Dump fifteen pounds of sand into a thick gardening garbage bag and tie it shut. Put that bag into the military duffle bag and you have your training implement! As you progress further into this training program, your sandbag will get heavier and heavier. With it, you will get increasingly stronger.

**P.S.** Grip strength leads to domination in anything that requires hand manipulation. Basketball players that are strong with the ball are the ones that do not have it taken from them. To build basketball grip strength, you need to first be able to handle a basketball. This means not only be able to dribble the ball but also receive it and be durable enough to deflect it without injury.

**Did You Know?** Slapping the basketball from hand to hand is an effective way to build shock absorbing qualities to your lower arms. This serves as injury preventive, strengthening, and conditioning purposes.

## PHASE II, COURSE II

Swamp lunges with bag in bear hug position using medium stride length.

I advocate a no more than a fifteen-pound increase in weighted resistance for this exercise. You can progress safely to a weight of twenty-five pounds after you can complete the long stride for distances over one hundred yards consistently.

1. Bear hug bag tightly.
2. High knee and fully extend one leg to the diagonal.
3. Land on heel to absorb body's force.
4. Turn and pivot back foot forwards on ball of foot.
5. Allow body to lean forward into a full lunge smoothly.
6. Just before knee touches the court push off front heel only.
7. Maintain erect back posture.
8. High knee and fully extend opposite leg to repeat process.

From this point further, I am going to refer to the added weighted resistance as the "bag."

Repeat until form failure. You are rocking' and rolling' at this point in training. A medium stride with a bag is tops work. Your form at this point should be smooth as butter left on the table. Everything you do is smooth because that's how you need to move.

Keep using your hands to crush and squeeze the bag. You can also crush and manipulate the bag with your wrists. This application has some historical significance to it. Well before the early 1900's strongmen used bags & barrels of flour, cement, hemp, beer etc. in order to physically train. Squeeze the bags and develop intense crushing power. Coordinate it with your breathing.

A bag in bear hug position gives the practitioner the opportunity to improve his chest and arm crushing power. When we talk about the application for a basketball player; we use an object that weighs more than a basketball. This object also has increased moveable quality and is multidimensional. When you train with a bear hug position with a bag, you are teaching yourself to never let go of the basketball. Your hands will be strong on the ball in time. Coaches want players to be strong with the ball.

A strong with the ball basketball player is one who can be dependable with the rock. This is essentially a player that the coach really trusts most because he knows that the player will make sound decisions under pressure. That leads me to my next important point; the player who remains calm and delivers what is necessary will win.

Hours of skill related drills, basketball practice, and this training will allow you to be strong with the ball. Once you can handle a basketball without ever having to look at it, you are comfortable. Once you are comfortable, now you need to work on your deception. The swamp lunges in your training have given you increases and confidence in your stride lengths. Now you can use that gained advantage for yourself on the court. You will feel a drastic difference in the way your legs functionally work after you begin training. Once you master the incorporation of your breathing, you will be one step closer to absolute physical mastery.

**P.S.** The maravich ball handling drills were the cornerstone of my own personal development. I started with the stationary drills and then progressed to the moving drills.

## PHASE II, COURSE III (OPTIMAL FLEXIBILITY)

I advocate a no more than a fifteen-pound increase in weighted resistance for this exercise. You can progress safely to a weight of twenty-five pounds after you can complete the long stride for distances over one hundred yards consistently.

1. Bear hug bag tightly.
2. High knee and fully extend one leg to the diagonal.
3. Land on heel to absorb body's force.
4. Turn and pivot back foot forwards on the ball of foot.
5. Allow body to lean forward into a full lunge smoothly.
6. Just before knee touches the court push off from heel only.
7. Maintain erect back posture.
8. High knee and fully extend opposite leg to repeat process.

Repeat until form is lost. I challenge you to take your swamp lunges for one hundred yards. Complete the one hundred yards in the best form you can use. In short; perfect. Remember that proper practice produces proper results.

When you can complete one hundred yards with a bag bear hugged your legs are really working. You should expect to have a tremendous increase in overall lower ability. With consistency I would guess that an average player could reach this point in three to four months.

Your lower body is optimally flexible at this point and highly resistant to any injury. This training is specifically injury preventative with unlimited benefits. If you open up the hips the rest of the lower body can be used in the fashion of which it was created.

Remember that when your stride length goes long, so do your actual walking, jogging, running strides. This improvement of flexibility affects all of your movement making you faster and more physically able. At this point, you know how this feels and it's great! There is no better feeling than having powerful legs that never get tired. Not to mention a pair of lungs to go with it and an upper body always ready.

Try explosively bear hugging with each stride taken. Always hold the bag but actually pulsate it by crushing it with hands on each stride. I would alternate hands with the pulsations exactly the same way you have done with your palm strikes. If you stride right, pulsate left.

Your upper body should be upright with the chest held in what could be called an "overconfident position". This represents maintaining and developing vertebral stability. Since our backs are our physical nemesis, we should improve its function directly. Keeping posture increases postural development which has been dubbed as "core strength".

## PHASE II, COURSE IV (OPTIMAL FLEXIBILITY + RESISTANCE)

Swamp lunges with bag in bear hug position, long stride length & leaning forward over front knee. I advocate a no more than a fifteen-pound increase in weighted resistance for this exercise. You can progress safely to a weight of twenty-five pounds after you can complete the long stride for distances over one hundred yards consistently.

1. Bear hug bag tightly.
2. High knee and fully extend one leg to the diagonal.
3. Land on heel to absorb body's force.
4. Turn and pivot back foot forwards on the ball of foot.
5. Allow body to lean forward into a full lunge smoothly.
6. Just before knee touches the court push off front heel only.
7. High knee and fully extend opposite leg to repeat process.

Repeat until form is lost. I have heard athletes call this exercise, "hell on wheels". Now when a professional athlete calls a fifteen pound bag "hell", I know we are onto something. This forward lean will again stretch the vertebral column dynamically.

The spinal flexion, extension, and torsion are a tremendous valued addition to this exercise. As stated previously, each time a bag is added, the leveraged can be changed by altering its positioning. All of these powerbag progressions are based on the laws of leverage in relation to gravity. These laws affect all of us on Earth.

As stated in the bodyweight phase, this is a time when you slowly add dimension into this training. I would advise smooth core twisting with each stride. This new dimension adds torsion across a plan you can and will work within during any basketball activity. Expect to flow smoothly with each twist and only move within your range.

There will never be a reason to push a joint past its natural resistance in training. Your flexibility will develop naturally over time with the right kind of work. Core torsion is now different. This core torsion will allow you to use more of your lower body power. The constant turning and pivoting of the back foot during the swamp lunge teaches motor memory to generate maximum lower body power.

Keep your torsion across a plane that is across several planes. You don't want to practice only one way to twist at the waist. Since you will be expected to suddenly react and twist randomly in a basketball game, you should do something similar in training. Now you are. With each stride, flow smoothly into it and twist. Once your next stride begins, flow smoothly into it and twist. Your strides should be as smooth as walking so you will never be in an uncomfortable position.

**P.S.** Swamp lunges with core torsion replace sit-ups forever!

# PHASE II CHALLENGE

I have trained alongside the finest Professionals in the world. In Portugal, I had a unique opportunity to train with Professional Soccer (Futbol), Beach Volleyball, Handball and of course, Basketball Players. I know what it takes to train as a Professional Athlete no matter what sport you dominate in. This next swamp lunge bag challenge is something that will knock your socks off. Right now, you are becoming incredibly durable within your entire body. This is evident of your mastery with the swamp lunge. At this point, the overall conditioning aspect of the swamp lunge has to have you thinking about training in general. I mean, how could one exercise applied with leverage principles do this much? The secret in the swamp lunge is that is teaches proper forward and diagonal movement. The planes you will cross allow your joints to flow during exercise. As you become more flexible, your strides increase. Once your strides increase, your flexibility has improved. This process continues until a point of optimal flexibility. Take a good look at the stride I take in the picture below. I can tell you that my current level of fitness with the swamp lunge allows me to move as fast as a quick walk. My body is conditioned for that movement. It is important that you realize how long it takes to develop that. In short; in time & patience. Your challenge is to take that bag and bang out one hundred and fifteen yards. You can pause if you need to and apply the same list of principles as in the Phase I Challenge. Once you add a fifteen pound powerbag all hell breaks loose. It is amazing what fifteen pounds can add. We feel that mere completion of this task is enough. Once you can complete this task easily you can move on to Phase III. Swamp lunge and mentally assess yourself. See if you can deliver some serious effort based training to yourself. Make your strides smooth, rhythmic, and consistent. Push yourself hard to make to it happen for yourself. Breaking the three-minute barrier is paramount training. Once you're below the two minute marker you are approaching incredible feats.

At left, you can see me executing a slam dunk with a fifteen pound bag. This is a demonstration of the vertical leap which basketball enthusiasts understand as the measurement of lower body power. You obviously need to keep your focus progressive and by that I mean concentrate on dunking a basketball first. A fifteen-pound bag weighs significantly more than a regulation sized basketball. I began using the bags in my skills training and it allowed me to progress to this point. I would also use the fifteen pound bag for my skill development in using the one on one offensive moves. I also replace the basketball with the bag for my entire stationary ball handling exercises, as you will see in great detail with Basketball Strength Volume II. I have made a regular workout of fifty dunks with the fifteen pound powerbag. It definitely is a gritty situation but it's one that I consistently grow from. I perform a fifty dunk drill with the bag once a month. (Photo by Joan Lemanczyk)

# PHASE III

## PHASE III, COURSE I

Swamp lunges with bag on one shoulder using short stride length. I advocate a no more than a fifteen pound increase in weighted resistance for this exercise. You can progress safely to a weight of twenty-five pounds after you can complete the long stride for distances over one hundred yards consistently. You are now applying the very principles of leverage and physics to our basketball training. When the bag is on your shoulder, it increases the tension on your stabilizing core muscles. You have altered the exercise by changing the weighted resistance. This tension on the shoulder represents a leverage disadvantage. Once the bags on your shoulder, you'll understand why this course recommends the bear hug version first.

1. Place bag on one shoulder and hold with both hands.
2. High knee and fully extend one leg to the diagonal.
3. Land on heel to absorb body's force.
4. Turn and pivot back foot forwards on the ball of foot.
5. Allow body to lean forward into a full lunge smoothly.
6. Just before knee touches the court push off front heel only.
7. Maintain erect back posture.
8. High knee and fully extend opposite leg to repeat process.

Repeat until form is lost, rest, and then repeat with bag on opposite shoulder. You want to take two solid runs at this. You only take each specific task with smoothness in mind. You know that by keeping your pace smooth and rhythmic that you earn results in time.

You will begin to experience increase within your core muscles in a very short period of time with this addition to the swamp lunge. At this point you already have plenty of quality time in training and know what patience brings.

Lastly as a friendly reminder, once we increase the tension using resistance, we always revert to the short stride length. A power bag on top of a shoulder represents an increase in exercise resistance. The stress is placed onto the lower body during a swamp lunge. This is due to us creating a leverage disadvantage situation.

Strive to keep your core where it needs to be; accommodating the exercise. Focus on keeping your rhythm and breathing consistent. Hold the bag with a firm grip and even pulsate it with each stride length. Your goal is to integrate as many variables as each situation in training allows. This is a sensible solution to physical training.

**P.S.** Shoulder the bag with each stride and watch the difference that makes! Keep switching the bag from shoulder to shoulder. The constant manipulation will fatigue your hands, shoulders, arms, and midsection.

## PHASE III, COURSE II

Swamp lunges with bag on one shoulder using medium stride length. I advocate a no more than a fifteen pound increase in weighted resistance for this exercise. You can progress safely to a weight of twenty-five pounds after you can complete the long stride for distances over one hundred yards consistently. Medium stride length time is a lot of fun. By now, you know when it's medium time, progress is coming quickly.

1. Place bag on one shoulder and hold with both hands.
2. High knee and fully extend one leg to the diagonal.
3. Land on heel to absorb body's force.
4. Turn and pivot back foot forwards on the ball of foot.
5. Allow body to lean forward into a full lunge smoothly.
6. Just before knee touches the court push off front heel only.
7. Maintain erect back posture.
8. High knee and fully extend opposite leg to repeat process.

Repeat until form is lost, rest, and then repeat with bag on opposite shoulder. Focus on contracting your abdominals and back muscles with each stride. You can do this with each breath you take. You need to contract your abdominal muscles as often and as consistent as possible.

The real trick is to always keep your abdominals tight while breathing and developing lung power. Everything in time, trust me. For now, inhale deeply, breathe out and contract. When you contract your abdominal muscles you should be landing on your front heel in a swamp lunge. Work your exhale of breath on your landing.

Coordinate the flexion of both hands on the bags with each breath. You should develop your ability to grab the bags quickly just like the claw of a crab. Dig your fingers into the bag and tap into your finger conditioning. These lower arm conditioning benefit a basketball player greatly. This makes the strong with the ball player in sure time.

I can't promise that a player will be able to make sound decisions under pressure with this phase but I can promise that he/she will physically be strong with the ball. Every single aspect of his game will improve. Remember, the lung power never ceases its development in training.

Once the breath is gone, so is the activity. If the breath is held the activity continues. This is again why building the foundation of lung power is so important. The flow of air into our bodies enables us to perform our required tasks. Without the air, we perish. Use the air that is free to your advantage and build your capacity to receive and expel it. I strongly advise you training in an environment that has clean air.

If you live in a populated area, rise early before others and train then. Most businesses are legally not allowed to begin until a specific time. Use that legality to your advantage, rise early and train before the pollution begins. This is much of the reason that I train outside and in close contact with nature.

## PHASE III, COURSE III (OPTIMAL FLEXIBILITY)

Swamp lunges with bag on one shoulder using long stride length. I advocate a no more than a fifteen-pound increase in weighted resistance for this exercise. You can progress safely to a weight of twenty-five pounds after you can complete the long stride for distances over one hundred yards consistently.

1. Place bag on one shoulder and hold with both hands.
2. High knee and fully extend one leg to the diagonal.
3. Land on heel to absorb body's force.
4. Turn and pivot back foot forwards on the ball of foot.
5. Allow body to lean forward into a full lunge smoothly.
6. Just before knee touches the court push off front heel only.
7. Maintain erect back posture.
8. High knee and fully extend opposite leg to repeat process.

Repeat until form failure, rest, and then repeat with bag on opposite shoulder. Do you remember when I wrote about how the tension is increased tremendously with long strides? You will understand all you need to know about leverage when you perform this exercise.

A good challenge with the long strider is a one hundred yard continual swamp lunge. If you can go one hundred strides, without stopping or pausing while having a powerbag on your shoulder, you're an animal.

Obviously, once you can conquer a hundred yards, move onto longer distances. The focus is always on the execution but you will become so efficient challenges will deem necessary. Take each challenge with pride and respect.

**P.S.** Try throwing smooth palm strikes while the bag is on the opposite shoulder. Why not do switch the bag onto the other shoulder after fifty strides/strikes and then finish the one hundred?

# PHASE III, COURSE IV (OPTIMAL FLEXIBILITY + RESISTANCE)

Swamp lunges with bag on one shoulder, using long stride length & leaning forward over front knee. I advocate a no more than a fifteen pound increase in weighted resistance for this exercise. You can progress safely to a weight of twenty-five pounds after you can complete the long stride for distances over one hundred yards consistently. Increase weight to a twenty-five pound powerbag after one month of consistent training.

1. Place bag on one shoulder and hold with both hands.
2. High knee and fully extend one leg to the diagonal.
3. Land on heel to absorb body's force.
4. Turn and pivot back foot forwards on the ball of foot.
5. Allow body to lean forward into a full lunge smoothly.
6. Just before knee touches the court push off front heel only.
7. High knee and fully extend opposite leg to repeat process.

As stated previously, the swamp lunge is an active dynamic stretch turned functional task for basketball players. The execution of the swamp lunge is a forward traveling diagonal lunge with added modifications for basketball players.

Since the game of basketball is one of constant surprise isometric/dynamic movement the swamp lunge consistently moves forward in a zigzag pattern. The zigzag pattern is much like the actual game of basketball. This will improve your ability to move within the game. The essence of sports training is to prepare athletes for competition. That is exactly what is going on right here, right now.

How often have you watched a basketball game where the players ran in perfectly straight lines? I have still never seen this happen. This is not a one-hundred-meter race.

The swamp lunge is a functional task that I devised in Junior College. It is one that took me from being a good basketball player/athlete to a very high level player/athlete with time and patience. We are a lot more alike that you may realize. It can happen for you!

This practice of traveling hamstring, glutei and hip dynamic stretching will enable you to reach what is known as the optimal flexibility, as stated previously. This has basketball player written all over it and that is exactly what you are.

Lastly, add core torsion to this application. Keep the progressions consistent and sensible. Since the leverage of the powerbag has changed the execution will feel slightly different. I can tell you by experience that it is a bit more difficult. It is very important to remember to flow smoothly into each movement.

**P.S.** It is crucial that you develop optimal flexibility with all of these various degrees of difficulty. The tension on the joints is greater and smaller depending on the particular movement. Its variance creates a unique learning experience through training.

# PHASE III CHALLENGE

Nice work so far, you are worthy of commending. We both know that this kind of training is what we were truly meant for. The basis of movement and building strength goes much deeper than what is commonly characterized as "exercise". I bet you're starting to wonder how something as simple as this can be so beneficial. The truth is in the application. Instructors who can "do" are essentially the bridges of information to anyone who currently isn't "doing". In order to be a good coach, one must give all the necessary information to be in a position to succeed. This is why I give you exactly what I give you and why. This is why I had asked you to master this type of movement and why it leads up to this next challenge. This next challenge is one you are ready for. I know you are ready because you have developed your short, medium and long stride lengths to a "T".

Take the bag and shoulder it. Swamp lunge one hundred yards with it on the original shoulder. Now, switch shoulders for the last one hundred yards of the swamp lunge. If you look for a further progression of the Phase III Challenge try switching the bag from shoulder to shoulder with each stride. This constant core torsion really works the entire body hard. As always, keep the breathing rhythmic and consistent. These challenges will teach you a lot about yourself and in regards to your potential through this movement. A fifteen pound point of resistance on TOP of the shoulder is going to do wonders for your abdominal and lower back region. You are also at the point where you have evolved as a being. Your movement during daily life has improved so much it must feel like your almost floating over the Earth. Your improved ability to travel up and down stairs is surprising isn't it? Once you can smack down two hundred yards simply go for more. You have no limits unless you place them on yourself. Always keep in mind that there is no limit. Simply, perform your training properly and your body will be ready to accept the demands you place upon it in time.

At left, you can see me on the free throw line during a professional game. For my entire basketball career, I shot over eighty percent from the free throw line. Making free throws is no secret. I learned to practice sprinting & then taking free throws. A simple drill you can implement is as follows. Start with your feet touching the baseline with the ball in hand. Dribble, sprint down the court & back peddle back to the baseline you started from. Now take a pair of free throws. Make or miss after the second free throw you need to get back to the baseline with the basketball. Now dribble, sprint down, back peddle back & sprint ANOTHER length of the court. After three sprints, take another pair of free throws. Each time you take a pair of free throws, you must increase one full court length of sprinting. Ten minutes of this is excellent free throw conditioning with tremendous game time carryover. We sprint forward and back peddle backwards because that's how basketball players move. I integrate the ball handling aspect because it is sensible. Perform this drill ten minutes a day. (Photo by Joao Freitas)

# PHASE IV

## PHASE IV, COURSE I

Swamp lunges with bags held on both shoulders with hands, using short stride length. I advocate two fifteen pound bags in weighted resistance for this exercise. You can progress safely to a weight of twenty-five pounds after you can complete the long stride for distances over one hundred yards consistently. In time, if you want an added option, increase the resistance to two, twenty-five pound powerbags after one month of consistent training.

1. Place bags on both shoulders, supporting them both hands.
2. High knee and fully extend one leg to the diagonal.
3. Land on heel to absorb body's force.
4. Turn and pivot back foot forwards on the ball of foot.
5. Allow body to lean forward into a full lunge smoothly.
6. Just before knee touches the court push off front heel only.
7. Maintain erect back posture.
8. High knee and fully extend opposite leg to repeat process.

Repeat until form is lost. Having a bag on each shoulder will actually feel easier for your core section. At this point in your training it is a welcomed element. The rules are still the same and there's only one way to do things; the right way with integrity.

The core stabilization required to make this exercise flow is astounding. There is simply no escape from the reality that the midsection ties the entire body together like glue. The stronger and more durable an athlete's midsection is the more resistant to injury and impressive he will be.

The progression from one bag to two bags will also be a rude awakening.

## PHASE IV, COURSE II

Swamp lunges with bags held on both shoulders with hands, using medium stride length. I advocate two fifteen pound bags in weighted resistance for this exercise. You can progress safely to a weight of twenty-five pounds after you can complete the long stride for distances over one hundred yards consistently. Increase weight to two, twenty-five pound powerbags after one month of consistent training.

1. Place bags on both shoulders, supporting them both with hands.
2. High knee and fully extend one leg to the diagonal.
3. Land on heel to absorb body's force.
4. Turn and pivot back foot forwards on the ball of foot.
5. Allow body to lean forward into a full lunge smoothly.
6. Just before knee touches the court push off front heel only.
7. Maintain erect back posture.
8. High knee and fully extend opposite leg to repeat process.

Repeat until form failure. Do not allow yourself to become part of any situation. Keep your focus on your breathing and physical execution. Nothing should get in the way of that. Once your focus/execution has been broken, you're done.

Alternate your hand flexion (pulsation) with each stride and breath. We're always looking to develop strength and conditioning with everything we do. You also want to concentrate on contracting your abdominals with each inhale and exhale. A lot has to be said for building abdominal muscles that can absorb impact.

When a player consistently works on contracting his abdominal section while breathing deeply, he builds much more than just lung power. The conditioning of the core is paramount to a basketball players overall movement. This is a very important next step of development in the player you can become. As a general rule, keep your core tight as if you were going to brace for a punch to the stomach. Your lung power development up until this point has prepared you for this.

If you want to build your midsection even more, do some concentrated midsections work after a cardiovascular exercise session. For example, run three miles and then do five minutes of consistent sit-ups. It is truly amazing how training the midsection after cardio works.

## PHASE IV, COURSE III (OPTIMAL FLEXIBILITY)

Swamp lunges with bags held on both shoulders with hands, using long stride length. I advocate two fifteen pound bags in weighted resistance for this exercise. You can progress safely to a weight of twenty-five pounds after you can complete the long stride for distances over one hundred yards consistently. Increase weight to two, twenty-five pound powerbags after one month of consistent training.

1. Place bags on both shoulders, supporting them both with hands.
2. High knee and fully extend one leg to the diagonal.
3. Land on heel to absorb body's force.
4. Turn and pivot back foot forwards on the ball of foot.
5. Allow body to lean forward into a full lunge smoothly.
6. Just before knee touches the court push off front heel only.
7. Maintain erect back posture.
8. High knee and fully extend opposite leg to repeat process.

Repeat until form failure. When you're taking strides this long and deep, there are no surprises when it comes to notable progress. Having a bag on each shoulder gives you added stability which leads to confidence. There is no coincidence between the two factors in training and in life. Look to exploit these factors and use them to your advantage.

Coaches often look to players who "have it". What this means is that a player should be expected to learn and perfect his body for function. In order to perfect the body the right kind of physical instruction needs to be in place. This very training represents that as it builds exactly what is needed for a basketball player to improve on the court.

I never believed in anything more than a t shirt for a reward to a weight lifting champion who didn't perform on the court. I have had teammates like that before and I respect the effort for what it is. Truth be told, if the players would have concentrated an equal amount on skill related work, they would have been more successful. The key is finding and obtain a perfect balance between training and basketball skill work/ practice. As stated previously, once your body is fully recovered from a previous training session, you are cleared by me to train again.

**P.S.** Most people never listen to their own bodily experience. Keep in mind that things that work need to keep being done to keep working. Train once, rest, repair, and then train again. There is no reason to deviate from a plan that consistently works for the results you are looking for.

## PHASE IV, COURSE IV (OPTIMAL FLEXIBILITY + RESISTANCE)

Swamp lunges with bags held on both shoulders with hands, using long stride length & leaning over front knee. I advocate two fifteen pound bags in weighted resistance for this exercise. You can progress safely to a weight of twenty-five pounds after you can complete the long stride for distances over one hundred yards consistently. Increase weight to two, twenty-five pound powerbags after one month of consistent training.

1.  Place bags on both shoulders, supporting them both with hands.
2.  High knee and fully extend one leg to the diagonal.
3.  Land on heel to absorb body's force.
4.  Turn and pivot back foot forwards on the ball of foot.
5.  Allow body to lean forward into a full lunge smoothly.
6.  Just before knee touches the court push off front heel only.
7.  High knee and fully extend opposite leg to repeat process.

Repeat until form failure. This is going to be the ultimate test of you lower back endurance. Since it is the most vulnerable portion of the human anatomy, it must be conditioned properly. This is why we use lightweight powerbags and sensible applications.

Basketball players need the endurance feel of "game shape". You can only achieve that feeling with work that provides it. Expect to be tested, expect to persevere, and expect to succeed with this challenge before even thinking about anything else. Succeed in the now and let later be later.

Core torsion with two powerbags while swamp lunging is awesome. This is some of the most fun that I have in training and I have fun! A player can expect to develop his entire midsection to the highest degree with the added dimension of core torsion in the swamp lunge. Coordinate your breathing with your striding/torsion. The leverages will be altered once again due to the power bag placements. Keep it smooth and sensible for maximum time.

This optimal flexibility level will be the hardest in terms of absolute muscular failure. I have trained many athletes who take the option of increasing the weight of the bags to continue this particular course. For those athletes, I always recommend this specific course, power presses, and fungo pops for their training.

# PHASE IV CHALLENGE

The Phase IV Challenge has the phrase, "Man-Up" all over it. To date, you have completed the first three Phases. I can tell you that your completion of those Phases has already benefited you more than you may realize. You are mastering the human body in relation to one of the first principles of the universe; the law of gravity. This next challenge is an extension of the double shoulder swamp lunge. Back in the golden era of boxing, real boxers wanted to always be able to "go the distance" and now it's time for you to go the distance. Take the bags, place them on your shoulders and go for two hundred yards. At this point you know what kind of pace you need to set yourself in order to finish strongly.

These distances will prove their worth in time as you do them. Take your time and complete the task correctly. If two hundred yards is too easy for you then why not make it one quarter mile. The quarter mile swamp lunge is a tough task one it's own, when performed properly. The soreness that comes later is incredible. It is often referred to as D.O.M.S. which stands for delayed onset muscle soreness. If you add a couple powerbags over a long distance course, you're talking SERIOUS METABOLIC TRAINING! Your lung power will keep your core section strong and stable during the challenge. All the work you have put in through training will pay off here in tremendous ways.

At left, you can see a perfect example of the offensive triple threat position. This is the specific stance to maintain when you have the ball in front of a defender. With the triple threat you can dribble, pass, or shoot. I ask that you hold this stance for at least one minute per day. The more often you use this stance, the quicker you will be able to adapt to the imposed demands. You are dangerous in this stance. Basketball players should expect swamp lunge training to directly carry over to the hardwood as well. As a rehash, think about each moment after you sweep and take one dribble. What happens to the legs? When you stride outward to the diagonal the back foot turns and pivots to accommodate the movement. (Photo by Joan Lemanczyk)

## HELPFUL REMINDERS

Dynamic stretches are the way to go to "warm" the body up. A baller could use ten paces of a swamp lunge or jumping jacks for example. Just remember to "get warm" with dynamic methods. Dynamic stretching represents safe and moving flexibility improvers that are usually accommodated by participant perspiration.

A player's program is simple and hard. On off-training days, ballers must jump rope (early in the morning) after dynamic stretching, shooting/ball handling (after rope) and soak their bodies in contrast baths. I recommend thirty minutes cold and thirty minutes warm thereafter. One hour per day submerged in water will do wonders for the body (flotion). You must also maintain adequate hydration.

# PHASE V

## PHASE V, COURSE I

Swamp lunges with bag held out in front of body in full extension, using short stride length. I advocate a fifteen pound bag in weighted resistance for this exercise. You can progress safely to a weight of twenty-five pounds after you can complete the long stride for distances over one hundred yards consistently. Increase weight to a twenty-five pound bag after one month of consistent training.

1. Place bag in both hands firmly, out in front of body in full extension.
2. High knee and fully extend one leg to the diagonal.
3. Land on heel to absorb body's force.
4. Turn and pivot back foot forwards on the ball of foot.
5. Allow body to lean forward into a full lunge smoothly.
6. Just before knee touches the court push off front heel only.
7. Maintain erect back posture.
8. High knee and fully extend opposite leg to repeat process.

Repeat until form failure. The drill develops the proper neurological/physical connections needed to keep hands up on defense. This represents an opportunity for tremendous shoulder girdle improvement!

The upper body bag integration of Volume I will begin with isometric work. I favor the isometric work due to the need of a basketball player to keep his hands up and aware at all times. When a players hands are up, they can be in a passing lane to deflect a ball into space for advantage. When a players hands are up they are in the vision of an offensive players. You can build absolute conditioning with a fifteen pound powerbag.

As a player, I respected defensive players with active, durable and powerful hands. Those hands were connected to shoulders that looked strong were even stronger. You need that look and that feel. To get that for the court, begin this shoulder girdle improvement. Keep your shoulder girdle in a strong, compact position.

Work as long as you can until your arms are no longer perpendicular with the ground. Your arms will fail before your legs due to your experience in training. Once your arms fail, continue to swamp lunge until your legs reach momentary muscular failure. Then, it's shut down time for this exercise for "x" training day. These rules are in place to ensure you truly learn your own physical training schedule as opposed to a documented schedule.

**P.S.** You can also stride and press the bag instead of the isometric start. You can even change the angle you press the bag at. I advise you to try different things and learn what you need the most help improving.

**When you "go by feel",
you make insurmountable progress.**

## PHASE V, COURSE II

Swamp lunges with bag held out in front of body in full extension, using medium stride length. I advocate a fifteen pound bag in weighted resistance for this exercise. You can progress safely to a weight of twenty-five pounds after you can complete the long stride for distances over one hundred yards consistently. Increase weight to a twenty-five pound bag after one month of consistent training.

1. Place bag in both hands firmly, out in front of body in full extension.
2. High knee and fully extend one leg to the diagonal.
3. Land on heel to absorb body's force.
4. Turn and pivot back foot forwards on the ball of foot.
5. Allow body to lean forward into a full lunge smoothly.
6. Just before knee touches the court push off front heel only.
7. Maintain erect back posture.
8. High knee and fully extend opposite leg to repeat process.

Repeat until form failure. Your grip and lower back conditioning will be noteworthy here. Your shoulder girdle is adapting to the stress imposed upon it. A principle relied upon in strength and conditioning science is the S.A.I.D. principle. This stands for.

S  Specific
A  Adaptation
I   Imposed
D  Demands

This principle applied means your body will adapt to almost anything if you do it sensibly and adequately care for yourself outside of the activity. Use this entire Volume I system and allow your body to adapt to it. With the proper care of the body, progress is unlimited and based on the participant's effort.

The longer your strides are, the longer your presses and pulls should be. This is a total body coordinated effort that begins first as an isometric and progresses into a functional isotonic exercise. Try to keep simultaneously timing the swamp lunges and the presses.

**P.S.** What good is a bench press if the game of basketball is played on two feet or in the air?

## PHASE V, COURSE III (OPTIMAL FLEXIBILITY)

Swamp lunges with bag held out in front of body in full extension, using long stride length. I advocate a fifteen pound bag in weighted resistance for this exercise. You can progress safely to a weight of twenty-five pounds after you can complete the long stride for distances over one hundred yards consistently. Increase weight to a twenty-five pound powerbag after one month of consistent training.

1. Place bag in both hands firmly, out in front of body in full extension.
2. High knee and fully extend one leg to the diagonal
3. Land on heel to absorb body's force.
4. Turn and pivot back foot forwards on the ball of foot.
5. Allow body to lean forward into a full lunge smoothly.
6. Just before knee touches the court push off front heel only.
7. Maintain erect back posture.
8. High knee and fully extend opposite leg to repeat process.

Repeat until form failure. That's it, hold that bag out as far as you can hold it. This isometric game is one of shear mental games. You might be surprised how long you can actually hold that bag once you begin concentrating on your breathing. Always remember; where there is full breath, there is an opportunity for major physicality.

Once you can no longer hold the bag, begin pushing/pulling it with each stride, as stated previously. You MUST work hard and smart and once again this represents that. Just because you can not HOLD the first position doesn't mean the exercise ends then. You simply adapt the exercise and continue it.

Just like the S.A.I.D. principle you must apply it again and again to yourself within sensible parameters. Those parameters are pushing and pulling the powerbag after your isometrics are completed. This is also a precursor to the power press. The power press is an excellent exercise progression that we will tend to shortly. Essentially, it is another progression of the palm strike but with a bag application. The movement is still relatively the same through the sagittal plane. Work hard and stay within yourself.

BASKETBALL STRENGTH | 99

## PHASE V, COURSE IV (OPTIMAL FLEXIBILITY + RESISTANCE)

Swamp lunges with bag held out in front of body in full extension, using long stride length & leaning over front knee. I advocate a fifteen-pound bag in weighted resistance for this exercise. You can progress safely to a weight of twenty-five pounds after you can complete the long stride for distances over one hundred yards consistently. Increase weight to a twenty-five-pound bag after one month of consistent training.

1. Place bag in both hands firmly, out in front of body in full extension.
2. High knee and fully extend one leg to the diagonal.
3. Land on heel to absorb body's force.
4. Turn and pivot back foot forwards on the ball of foot.
5. Allow body to lean forward into a full lunge smoothly.
6. Just before knee touches the court push off front heel only.
7. High knee and fully extend opposite leg to repeat process.

Repeat until form is lost. You shoulder girdle conditioning must be tremendous if you are at this point of training. At this point you are enjoying the pushing and pulling challenge after your isometrics fail. This second calling of your shoulder girdle will help properly condition you for competition. You need to improve both pushing and pulling motions equally.

Using a bag, you can use a resistance that you can naturally progress with. You can only press as hard as you can pull backwards. At the same time, you must concentrate on your swamp lunge strides. By now, there is a lot going on without there really being a lot going on. This is all progressive, first the swamp lunge, isometrics and now progressive power presses. All this must make sense to work and that is exactly why it works.

Your pushes and pulls develop the corresponding soft tissues of the entire upper body. If pushing and pulling becomes to tiring before your legs fatigue, mix in some shrugs. With each stride shrug your shoulders up and back then down. Shoulder girdle elevation is an important facet to improve. In a sense, shoulder girdle elevation is nothing more than a shrug up and back then down. The up and back movement is to ensure scapulae retraction.

This movement serves for injury prevention and function. The entire shoulder girdle, upper thoracic region, and cervical region depend upon conditioning developed through elevation. Protect your neck and keep working intelligently!

# POWER PRESSES

This challenge is unlike the previous four. This time, there is absolutely no application of the swamp lunge. I am confident that at this point, you have all the ammo you need within your lower body. It is important not to get greedy or become complacent once you find yourself in amazing shape. You still need to work hard every day to keep your consistency and raise your fitness level. The human body will adapt to almost anything if you give it a chance. This next challenge is the Power Press. This exercise is one that derives from the simple act of pushing then pulling. An athlete can simply step forward and push with both hands. In the game of basketball a chest pass is where this movement is highly recognized. Take your bag and grip it tight. Step forward with one foot and press the Powerbag to arms length ONLY to pull it backwards. You want to take this slowly and gradually build up your bodies conditioning. In time your Power Press will look ferocious and the strength you will have earned goes far and beyond any bench press. You understand that you are going to release and stop your own power. Now when you are comfortable with handling your own power go for the century. That is right, one hundred repetitions in the Power Press. I have benched over four hundred pounds and can say that power pressing thirty five is much more of a workout. The power presses have also enabled me to reach my explosive pushing power.

# PHASE VI

## PHASE VI, COURSE I

Swamp lunges with bag held pressed over head in full extension, using short stride length. I advocate a fifteen-pound bag in weighted resistance for this exercise. You can progress safely to a weight of twenty-five pounds after you can complete the long stride for distances over one hundred yards consistently. Increase weight to a twenty-five pound powerbag after one month of consistent training.

1. Place bag in hands firmly, press and hold over head in full extension.
2. High knee and fully extend one leg to the diagonal.
3. Land on heel to absorb body's force.
4. Turn and pivot back foot forwards on the ball of foot.
5. Allow body to lean forward into a full lunge smoothly.
6. Just before knee touches the court push off front heel only.
7. Maintain erect back posture.
8. High knee and fully extend opposite leg to repeat process.

Repeat until form failure. Hold this bag up and over your head for as long as you can. There is no reason to put this bag down at all. You are training right now and the bag needs to stay up.

Once the bag inevitably comes down, you need to begin overhead pressing it corresponding with each stride. You need to breathe with rhythm and power. Strive to keep your chest high and maintain vertebral stability. Building the postural muscles of the body can not be overlooked. Holding a position like this is not easy due to the core accentuation on postural muscles and tissues. That is the very reason why this is the last phase of the swamp lunge. Once the isometric overhead hold fails, the overhead pressing begins.

With each stride, press the bag overhead. The fifteen pound powerbag will seem like one hundred pounds in due time. I guarantee your amazement when that becomes a reality. Then at that specific point in time, you will come to full realization that you do not need heavy resistance to train effectively.

What you need is an effective plan and to execute it. Good coaches diagram strategies that can be executed by their players in successful fashion. Listening and following directions is the; be all, end all. Why not do the same in training? Everything that you do has to make sense and that's why I put Volume I together for you.

**P.S.** Overhead pressing during swamp lunges are very challenging therefore you must proceed with caution. There is a specific reason why this is the last phase of this training course.

## PHASE VI, COURSE II

Swamp lunges with bag held pressed over head in full extension, using medium stride length. I advocate a fifteen-pound bag in weighted resistance for this exercise. You can progress safely to a weight of twenty-five pounds after you can complete the long stride for distances over one hundred yards consistently. Increase weight to a twenty-five pound bag after one month of consistent training.

1. Place bag in hands firmly, press and hold over head in full extension.
2. High knee and fully extend one leg to the diagonal.
3. Land on heel to absorb body's force.
4. Turn and pivot back foot forwards on the ball of foot.
5. Allow body to lean forward into a full lunge smoothly.
6. Just before knee touches the court push off front heel only.
7. Maintain erect back posture.
8. High knee and fully extend opposite leg to repeat process.

Repeat until form failure. Right about now you are in a strong place. You can sit in low lunges, squats and perform upper body movements with no problem. You are an animal for real. Think about the things you can do that are similar to what impressive animals out in the wild can do. Think about how you have learned to move.

When you develop this type of conditioning, you are really building much more than basketball strength. You are becoming the most improved version of yourself you can hope to become. Keep the consistency and execute perfect practice. In time, you will receive perfect results.

## PHASE VI, COURSE III (OPTIMAL FLEXIBILITY)

Swamp lunges with bag held pressed over head in full extension, using long stride length. I advocate a fifteen pound bag in weighted resistance for this exercise. You can progress safely to a weight of twenty-five pounds after you can complete the long stride for distances over one hundred yards consistently. Increase weight to a twenty-five pound bag after one month of consistent training.

1. Place bag in hands firmly, press and hold over head in full extension.
2. High knee and fully extend one leg to the diagonal.
3. Land on heel to absorb body's force.
4. Turn and pivot back foot forwards on the ball of foot.
5. Allow body to lean forward into a full lunge smoothly.
6. Just before knee touches the court push off front heel only.
7. Maintain erect back posture.
8. High knee and fully extend opposite leg to repeat process.

Repeat until form failure. This is the most difficult variation of the swamp lunge and for good reason. The spinal flexion and overhead hold is a very difficult position to hold. You have been prepared for this with all of your training to this point. Your core is conditioned from all of your bodyweight training and powerbag leverage progressions.

**Take what's yours because
no one is going to serve it up to you!**

## PHASE VI, COURSE IV (OPTIMAL FLEXIBILITY + RESISTANCE)

Swamp lunges with bag held pressed over head in full extension, using long stride length & leaning body over front knee. I advocate a fifteen pound bag in weighted resistance for this exercise. You can progress safely to a weight of twenty-five pounds after you can complete the long stride for distances over one hundred yards consistently. Increase weight to a twenty-five pound bag after one month of consistent training.

1. Place bag in hands firmly, press and hold over head and hold in extension.
2. High knee and fully extend one leg to the diagonal.
3. Land on heel to absorb body's force.
4. Turn and pivot back foot forwards on the ball of foot.
5. Allow body to lean forward into a full lunge smoothly.
6. Just before knee touches the court push off front heel only.
7. High knee and fully extend opposite leg to repeat process.

Repeat until form failure. This is it, the last and final phase of the swamp lunge. If you are at this point in training, it is hard for me to believe that you could be physically beat on the basketball court. The shear endurance and mental toughness required to train this way consistently is tremendous. There is a special place in my heart for each and every player who is willing to sacrifice their personal time and physical body in order to improve. Essentially, that is what it takes to be the best at anything.

Keep in mind the lessons you learn from training session to session. Another suggestion I have for you is to keep a simple training journal. Include statistics like stride lengths, total repetitions and most importantly time under tension. Your overall goal is to be able to train for an infinite amount of time. Set your mind this way and you might be surprised what happens to you.

Your training records should also contain actual key feelings of the training. Use adjectives to detail how you felt coming into training, during and definitely after. Keeping records like this allows you to completely remember the experience without ever losing the essence of it. Since the brain is a super computer that works off fed information, you can feed your past experience back to yourself for later evaluation.

# FUNGO POPS

The word Fungo (as you as you all know) means alone or by yourself. The word pop refers to the sound of delivery when you strike an object. Put the two together with a powerbag and you have a phenomenal combination. This exercise allows you to build force absorption quality in your wrists. The footwork associated with the Fungo Pop is important. Step forward to strike forward. Step to the side to strike to the side. Throw the Powerbag in front of you, step forward and palm strike the bag. Keep it simple.

## KEEP YOUR THUMB OUTWARD AND TO THE SIDE

This exercise is hand/eye accuracy at its finest. The Fungo Pop is generating maximum force (striking) and force absorbing (grabbing). When performed correctly by an advanced practitioner this exercise is scary from the right set of eyes. Take a fifteen pound Powerbag and knock off fifty pops. This workout will prove its worth in a very short period of time.

After you have completed this task, think about how powerful you will become in time. I can tell you from experience that it feels good to know what you are capable of. In time, your sagittal striking power will become so great that this exercise will be all about pain tolerance. The explosive qualities that you can build from this exercise are unlimited.

## Maurice Bailey Fungo Pops

## Bryan Bailey Fungo Pops

# CLOSURE

Congratulations, you have just completed reading Basketball Strength Volume I. My intention with this training course was to provide you with the most comprehensive, progressive and confidence building formula for your eventual basketball success. You should know that I am interested in your progress. It is with great pleasure that I can say that you have the information you need to begin your basketball conditioning RIGHT NOW! This actual doing will be the best physical preparing you ever do for the sport of basketball. The swamp lunge progressions, power presses and fungo pops will allow you to develop serious all around basketball strength. It will make you a better player. The first thing you must do when you are ready to train for your first time is to properly assess yourself. A golden rule is to always start from the bottom and work your way up. Take short strides and develop them to a point of total fluidity. Follow each course and phase. You will know when you are ready to slowly start inching out and increasing the strides. A one inch increase in a stride can represent a mountain of difference. This is why the progressions exist. Remember to take your time and develop. Take your palm strikes, power presses, overhead presses, core torsions, and fungo pop progressions as carefully as your swamp lunges. The principles of proper exercise development apply to all aspects of training. Once you build your ability to perform the movements correctly, your stamina and strength will have already improved. This will allow you to become more on the basketball court. Keep practicing and doing only what is physically required. This ensures your ability to generate the maximum into all tasks. Concentrate on your breathing because when your breath is lost, so are you. Once again lung power must be a priority. I am a firm believer in the benefits of lung power development. Basketball Strength Volume I contains the keys to open the doors of your physical mastery. I have carefully laid out progressions for you to ensure your eventual success. The usage of sports specific bags is paramount in reaching basketball ability. Using the bags instead of weights is the finest choice a coach can ever make for his athletes. Bags do not present the same dangers that traditional weightlifting presents. Obviously it is the instruction pertaining to any material that leads to success and failure but in the interest of brevity, here at Basketball Strength we keep it simple. We use our bodies and lightweight powerbags as resistance. We realize that it is our intention to improve as basketball players and not as weightlifters. As a reminder, remember to do your swamp lunges and keep the form smooth. When you dedicate yourself to learning this movement, you will literally watch yourself do things that you never thought possible. For example; I haven't played a professional basketball game in six years yet I maintain a level of fitness that allows me to still sky at least a foot and change over the rim (see cover photo). By now you know that there is a direct carryover from this training to the basketball court. Training with the bags gives you a tighter grip on the basketball whenever it is in my hands. I find that I am also able to find my stride to deliver explosiveness from anywhere on the court. This is something you will find out as well. Give me one dribble and I can take it strong to rim from outside the three point arc. These long strides are developed through swamp lunge progressions. You have the complete road map of basketball training now. In the last two phases you need to mix in power presses and overhead with your strides. The course asks for you to hold the bags in static extension and you should start that way. Once you become strong in this isometric fashion, begin using the power presses and overhead presses with each stride. A good workout is using a press for each stride. All of your presses should be as smooth as your swamp lunge strides. A cardinal rule of training is to learn to harness strengths and build weaknesses. Well, your lower body needs to be your strength and we will build your upper body. Now that you are working smart, results come in time. Your fungo pops allow you to build tremendous striking power. Since your hands are so vital to you, we have to have them in top condition. The fungo pops allow you to build necessary shock absorption preventing injuries. There is a lot to be said about the improvement of the lower arms for a basketball player. The fungo exercise allows a player to build his eye/hand accuracy while strengthening his body naturally. By naturally, I mean that you can only strike as hard as you can grab. If you strike the bag too hard and your hand strength is not compatible then you will drop that bag. You need to learn to use only what you need to use and don't drop it. Once you find that zone, begin striking beyond the bag and remember to breathe outward with each stride. The overall conditioning is tremendous not to mention its actual combat application. I have personally found that I can fungo pop a fifteen pound bag twenty to fifty times depending on my pain tolerance that day. I am at the point where I am palm striking the powerbags and there is a cloud of dust in the air. I begin and complete one set of fungo pops per work out and I will not use this exercise until soreness is completely gone. This process of healing for me is about three to four days. I won't train sore because I can wait the one more day to ensure maximum improvement. I know there is no prize for trying to be the workout hero and getting hurt. The reality here is that I train wisely and the time I spend healing is the time I spend improving. All of the food I eat and adequate rest I receive leads to my inevitable improvement. Now all these same rules will apply to you because I know you're willing to work. Dedicate yourself to learning yourself. With each training session is an opportunity to learn and improve many things about your self. Training is a physical outlet that everyone needs. Once that training is sensible and effort based, results come in time. You have that time because you can make it work for you starting RIGHT NOW! That's right, you have the plan, now put it into place and prepare to succeed.

Remember consistently visit my daily blog @ www.basketballstrength. com/blog for daily bits to keep your game live. Basketball Strength exists because the game needs it. The game needs a full proof method of metabolic conditioning that is effort based. The greatest thing about sensible effort based training is that the results are directly based on the acting participant. This represents an acceptance of personal responsibility and a path to independence. Begin this training as soon as possible. A perfect time to start is right now. Trust me when I say you can safely drop anything you are currently doing and do this. Do this because it is proven to work for just more than weight room heroics. My system of training improves the human being to move through several specific patterns over extended periods of time. My system of training also yields immediate results with your effort. Remember to stick to the principles of single exercise performance. There is no need for multiple sets of any exercise unless you are an advanced trainee embarking a challenge.

If you need a push to get you started, try this routine below. Assess yourself accordingly.

- Mountain Climbers      Perform until lather is achieved.
- Swamp lunges      Until form failure
- Fungo Pops      Twenty-five strikes per hand
- Defensive stance isometrics      Until form failure
- Power presses      Twenty-five presses
- Sit-Ups      Until form failure
- Rope Skipping      Perform until new lather is achieved

### Basketball Strength - Volume II coming soon!

# ABOUT THE AUTHOR

Dave has always had a fond love of basketball and physical training. He has committed his life to this pursuit of instruction. He played basketball as a Nassau Community College Lion for one year at small forward before accepting a basketball scholarship and transferring to the University of Bridgeport. For two consecutive basketball seasons under head coach Bruce Webster (1998-2000), David led the N.E.C.C. in rebounds per game despite being undersized at 6'-4". While at the University of Bridgeport, Dave established himself as an All-Conference and All-Northeast performer. In Dave's senior season (1999-2000) his talents were recognized by professional scouts both domestically and internationally. Upon graduation from the University of Bridgeport in 2000, David signed a contract to play Professional European Basketball (C.D. Nacional). This achievement represented a huge milestone for him and a continuance of the professional athletics family lineage. Dave played one year for C.D. Nacional located in Funchal, Madeira Island, Portugal. Lemanczyk averaged over twenty points and ten rebounds at the shooting guard position during his yearly stay. He would attend various free agent camps in the following three years (2001-2003) but would not sign another professional contract. In 2003, Dave decided to go back to school and earn a Master of Science in Physical Education from Hofstra University. Dave properly motivates, inspires and educates the mass of people looking for the truth to our human physicality. He does this through proper pedagogical progression in basketball training instruction (**BASKETBALL STRENGTH**).

Printed in the USA
CPSIA information can be obtained
at www.ICGtesting.com
LVHW011958310124
770343LV00001B/2